4/24

For Gra ♡

Enjoy! (If you can!)

Love,
Mom

of

g

SO-DFL-843

TERMINATOR PLANET

THE FIRST HISTORY OF DRONE WARFARE, 2001-2050

NICK TURSE
AND
TOM ENGELHARDT

Dispatch Books

Dispatch Books

Copyright 2012

All Rights Reserved

ISBN-13: 978-1477475942

ISBN-10: 147747594X

First Edition 2012

Table of Contents

Chapter 1: Filling the Skies With Assassins

Chapter 2: Droning On

Chapter 3: The Forty-Year Drone War

Chapter 4: The Perfect American Weapon

Chapter 5: Top Guns No More

Chapter 6: America's Secret Empire of Drone Bases

Chapter 7: Sex and the Single Drone

Chapter 8: The Life and Death of American Drones

Chapter 9: Offshore Everywhere

Chapter 10: The Crash and Burn Future of Robot Warfare

Chapter 11: Remotely Piloted War

Chapter 12: A Drone-Eat-Drone World

Postscript: America as a Shining Drone Upon a Hill

Chapter 1

Filling the Skies with Assassins

Tom Engelhardt

In 1984, Skynet, the supercomputer that rules a future Earth, sent a cyborg assassin, a "terminator," back to our time. His job was to liquidate the woman who would give birth to John Connor, the leader of the underground human resistance of Skynet's time. You with me so far? That, of course, was the plot of the first *Terminator* movie and for the multi-millions who saw it, the images of future machine war -- of hunter-killer drones flying above a wasted landscape -- are unforgettable.

Since then, as Hollywood's special effects took off, there were two sequels during which the original terminator somehow morphed into a friendlier figure on screen, and even more miraculously, off-screen, into the humanoid governor of California. In 2009, the fourth film in the series, *Terminator Salvation*, descended on us, hitting our scattered multiplexes.

Oh, sorry, I didn't mean *hit* hit. I meant, arrived in.

Meanwhile, hunter-killer drones weren't waiting for Hollywood. As you sat in that movie theater back in May 2009, actual unmanned aerial vehicles (UAVs), pilotless surveillance and assassination drones armed with Hellfire missiles, were already patrolling our expanding global battlefields, hunting down human beings. And in the Pentagon and the labs of defense contractors, UAV supporters were already talking about and working on next-generation machines. Post-2020, according to these dreamers, drones will be able to fly *and* fight, discern enemies *and* incinerate them without human decision-making. They're even wondering about just how to program human ethics, or at least American ethics, into them.

Okay, it may never happen, but it should still make you blink that out there in America are people eager to bring the next iteration of *Terminator* not to local multiplexes, but to the skies of our perfectly real world -- and that the Pentagon is already funding them to do so.

An Arms Race of One

Now, keep our present hunter-killer drones, those MQ-1 Predators and more advanced MQ-9 Reapers, in mind for a moment. Remember that, as you read, they're cruising Afghan and Pakistani skies looking for potential "targets," and in Pakistan's tribal borderlands, are employing what then Centcom commander (now CIA chief) General David Petraeus called "the right of last resort" to take out "threats" (as well as tribespeople who just happen to be in the vicinity). And bear with me while I offer you a little potted history of the modern arms race.

Think of it as starting in the early years of the twentieth century when Imperial Britain, industrial juggernaut and colonial upstart Germany, and Imperial Japan all began to plan and build new generations of massive battleships or dreadnoughts (followed by "super-dreadnoughts") and so joined in a fierce naval arms race. That race took a leap onto land and into the skies in World War I when scientists and war planners began churning out techno-marvels of death and destruction meant to break the stalemate of trench warfare on the Western front.

Each year, starting in 1915, new or improved weaponry -- poison gas, upgrades of the airplane, the tank and then the improved tank -- appeared on or above the battlefield. Even as those marvels arrived, the next generation of weapons was already on the drawing boards. (In a sense, American auto makers took up the same battle plan in peacetime, unveiling new, ramped up car models each year.) As a result, when World War I ended in 1918, the war machinery of 1919 and 1920 was already being mapped out and developed. The next war, that is, and the weapons that would go with it were already in the mind's eye of war planners.

From the first years of the twentieth century on, an obvious prerequisite for what would prove a never-ending arms race was two to four great powers in potential collision, each of which had the ability to mobilize scientists, engineers, universities, and manufacturing power on a massive scale. World War II was, in these terms, a bonanza for invention as well as destruction. It ended, of course, with the Manhattan Project, that *ne plus ultra* of industrial-sized invention for destruction, which produced the first atomic bomb, and the Cold War nuclear arms race that followed.

In that 45-year-long brush with extinction, the United States and the Soviet Union each mobilized a military-industrial complex to build ever newer generations of ever more devastating nuclear weaponry and delivery systems for a MAD (mutually assured destruction) world. At the peak of that two-superpower arms race, the resulting arsenals had the mad capacity to destroy eight or ten planets our size.

In 1991, after 73 years, the Soviet Union, that Evil Empire, simply evaporated, leaving a single superpower without rivals astride planet Earth. And then came the unexpected thing: the arms race, which had been almost a century in the making, did not end. Instead, the unimaginable occurred and it simply morphed into a "race" of one with a finish line so distant -- the bomber of 2018, Earth-spanning weapons systems, a vast anti-ballistic missile system, and weaponry for the heavens of perhaps 2050 -- as to imply eternity.

The Pentagon and the military-industrial complex surrounding it -- including mega-arms manufacturers, advanced weapons labs, university science centers, and the official or semi-official think tanks that churned out strategies for future military domination -- went right on. After a brief, post-Cold War blip of time in which "peace dividends" were discussed but not implemented, the "race" actually began to amp up again, and after September 11, 2001, went into overdrive against "Islamo-fascism" (aka the Global War on Terror, or the Long War).

In those years, our Evil Empire of the moment, except in the minds of a clutch of influential neocons, was a ragtag terrorist outfit made up of perhaps a few thousand adherents and scattered global wannabes, capable of mounting spectacular-looking but infrequent and surprisingly low-tech attacks on symbolic American (and other) targets. Against this enemy, the Pentagon budget became, for a while, an excuse for anything.

This brings us to our present unbalanced world of military might in which the U.S. accounts for nearly half of all global military spending and the total Pentagon budget is almost six times that of the next contender, China. In 2009, the Chinese announced relatively modest plans to build up their military and create a genuinely offshore navy. Similarly, the Russians moved to downsize and refinance their tattered armed forces and the industrial complex that goes with them, while upgrading their weapons systems. This could potentially make the country more competitive when it comes to global arms dealing, a market more than half of which has been cornered by the U.S. Nonetheless, the U.S. will remain in a futuristic arms race of one, a significant part of which involves reserving the skies for American power.

Assassination by Air

Speaking of controlling those skies, let's get back to UAVs. As futuristic weapons planning went, they started out pretty low-tech in the 1990s. Even today, the most commonplace of the two American armed drones, the Predator, costs only $4.5 million a pop, while the most advanced model, that Reaper -- both are produced by General Atomics Aeronautical Systems of San Diego -- comes in at $15 million. (Even counting development costs, ground equipment and other related expenses, which significantly raise the per-unit cost, compare that to $350 million for a single F-22 Raptor, which has proved essentially useless in America's most recent counterinsurgency wars.) It's lucky UAVs are cheap, since they are also prone to crashing. Think of them as snowmobiles with wings that have received ever more sophisticated optics and powerful weaponry.

They came to life as surveillance tools during the wars over the former Yugoslavia, were armed by February 2001, were hastily pressed into operation in Afghanistan after 9/11, and like many weapons systems, began to evolve generationally. As they did, they developed from surveillance eyes in the sky into something far more sinister and previously restricted to *terra firma*: assassins. One of the earliest armed acts of a CIA-piloted Predator, back in November 2002, was an assassination mission over Yemen in which a jeep, reputedly transporting six suspected al-Qaeda operatives, was obliterated .

Today, the most advanced UAV, the Reaper, housing up to four Hellfire missiles and two 500-pound bombs, packs the sort of punch once reserved for a jet fighter. Dispatched to the skies over the farthest reaches of the American empire, powered by a 1,000-horsepower turbo prop engine at its rear, the Reaper can fly at up to 21,000 feet for up to 22 hours (until fuel runs short), streaming back live footage from three cameras (or sending it to troops on the ground) --16,000 hours of video a month.

No need to worry about a pilot dozing off during those 22 hours. The human crews "piloting" the drones, often from thousands of miles away, just change shifts when tired. So the planes are left to endlessly cruise Afghan and Pakistani skies relentlessly seeking out, like so many terminators, specific enemies whose identities can, under certain circumstances -- or so the claims go -- be determined even through the walls of houses. When a "target" is found and agreed upon -- in Pakistan, the permission of Pakistani officials to fire is no longer considered necessary -- and a missile or bomb is unleashed, the cameras are so powerful that "pilots" can reputedly watch the facial expressions of those being liquidated on their computer monitors "as the bomb hits."

As of early 2009, approximately 5,500 UAVs, mostly unarmed -- less than 250 of them are Predators and Reapers -- operated over the Greater Middle East. Part of the more-than-century-long development of war in the air, drones have become favorites of American military planners. Robert Gates in particular as Secretary of Defense demanded increases in their production (and in the training of their pilots) and urged that they be rushed in quantity into America's battle zones even before being fully perfected.

And yet, keep in mind that the UAV still remains in its (frightening) infancy. Such machines are not, of course, advanced cyborgs. They are in some ways not even all that advanced. Because the Pentagon wanted publicity for the drone-war program during the late 2000s, reporters from the U.S. and elsewhere were given "rare behind-the-scenes" looks at how it worked. As a result, and also because the "covert war" in the skies over Pakistan made Washington's secret warriors proud enough to regularly leak news of its "successes," we know something about our drone wars.

We learned , for instance, that part of the Air Force's Afghan UAV program runs out of Kandahar Air Base in southern Afghanistan. It turns out that, pilotless as the planes may be, a pilot does have to be nearby to guide them into the air and handle landings. As soon as the drone is up, a two-man team, a pilot and a "sensor monitor," backed by intelligence experts and meteorologists, takes over the controls at stateside facilities like Davis-Monthan Air Force Base in Tucson, Arizona, or at Creech Air Force Base northwest of Las Vegas, some 7,000-odd miles away. (Other U.S. bases are involved as well.)

According to Christopher Drew of the *New York Times*, who, in 2009, visited Davis-Monthan where Air National Guard members handle the controls, the pilots sit unglamorously "at 1990s-style computer banks filled with screens, inside dimly lit trailers." Depending on the needs of the moment, they could find themselves "over" either Afghanistan or Iraq, or even both on the same work shift. All of this is remarkably mundane -- pilot complaints generally run to problems "transitioning" back to wife and children after a day at the joystick over battle zones -- and at the same time, right out of Ali Baba's *One Thousand and One Nights*.

In those dimly lit trailers, the UAV teams have taken on an almost godlike power. Their job is to survey a place thousands of miles distant (and completely alien to their lives and experiences), assess what they see, and spot "targets" to eliminate -- even if on their somewhat antiquated computer systems it "takes up to 17 steps -- including entering data into pull-down windows -- to fire a missile" and incinerate those below. They only face danger, other than carpal tunnel syndrome, when they leave the job. A sign at Creech warns pilots to "drive carefully"; this, it says, is "the most dangerous part of your day." Those involved claim that the fear and thrill of battle do not completely escape them, but the descriptions we now have of their world sound discomfortingly like a cross between the far frontiers of sci-fi and a call center in India.

The most intense of our various drone wars, the one on the other side of the Afghan border in Pakistan, is also the most mysterious. We know that some of the drones engaged in it take off from Pakistani airfields; that this "covert war" (which regularly makes front-page news) is run by the CIA out of its headquarters in Langley, Virginia; that its pilots are also located somewhere in the U.S.; and that at least some of them are hired private contractors.

William Saletan of *Slate* has described our drones as engaged in "a bloodless, all-seeing airborne hunting party." Of course, what was once an elite activity performed in person has been transformed into a 24/7 industrial activity fit for human drones.

Our drone wars also represent a new chapter in the history of assassination. Once upon a time, to be an assassin for a government was a furtive, shameful thing. In those days, of course, an assassin, if successful, took down a single person, not the targeted individual and anyone in the vicinity (or simply, if targeting intelligence proves wrong, anyone in the vicinity). No more poison-dart-tipped umbrellas, as in past KGB operations, or toxic cigars as in

CIA ones -- not now that assassination has taken to the skies as an everyday, all-year-round activity.

Today, we increasingly display our assassination wares with pride. To us, at least, it seems perfectly normal for assassination aerial operations to be a part of an open discussion in Washington and in the media. Consider this a new definition of "progress" in our world.

Proliferation and Sovereignty

This brings us back to arms races. They may be things of the past, but don't for a minute imagine that those hunter-killer skies won't someday fill with the drones of other nations. After all, one of the truths of our time is that no weapons system, no matter where first created, can be kept for long as private property. Today, we talk not of arms races, but of "proliferation," which is what you have once a global arms race of one takes hold.

In drone-world, the Chinese, the Russians, the Israelis, the Pakistanis, the Georgians, and the Iranians, among others, already have drones. In the Lebanon War of 2006, Hezbollah flew drones over Israel. In fact, if you have the skills, you can create your own drone, more or less in your living room (as your basic DIY drone website indicates). Undoubtedly, the future holds unnerving possibilities for small groups intent on assassination from the air.

Already the skies are growing more crowded. Soon after entering the Oval Office, President Obama issued what Reuters termed "an unprecedented videotaped appeal to Iran... offering a 'new beginning' of diplomatic engagement to turn the page on decades of U.S. policy toward America's longtime foe." It was in the form of a Persian New Year's greeting. As the *New York Times* also reported, the U.S. military beat the president to the punch. They sent their own "greetings" to the Iranians a couple of days earlier.

After considering what *Times* reporters Rod Nordland and Alissa J. Rubin termed "the delicacy of the incident at a time when the United States is seeking a thaw in its relations with Iran," the U.S. military sent out Col. James Hutton to meet the press and "confirm" that "allied aircraft" had shot down an "Iranian unmanned aerial vehicle" over Iraq on February 25, 2009, more than three weeks earlier. Between that day and mid-March, the relevant Iraqi military and civilian officials were, the *Times* tells us, not informed. The reason? At the time, that drone was intruding on our (borrowed) airspace, not theirs.

And naturally enough, we don't want other countries' drones in "our" airspace, though that's hardly likely to stop them. The Iranians, for instance, have already announced the development of "a new generation of 'spy drones' that provide real-time surveillance over enemy terrain."

Of course, when you openly control fleets of assassination drones patrolling airspace over other countries, you've already made a mockery of whatever national sovereignty might once have meant. It's a precedent that may someday even make us distinctly uncomfortable. But not right now.

If you doubt this, check out the stream of self-congratulatory comments being leaked by Washington officials about our drone assassins. These often lead off news pieces about America's "covert war" over Pakistan ("An intense, six-month campaign of Predator strikes in Pakistan has taken such a toll on Al Qaeda that militants have begun turning violently on one another out of confusion and distrust, U.S. intelligence and counter-terrorism officials say..."); but be sure to read to the end of such pieces. Somewhere in them, after the successes have been touted and toted up, you get the bad news: "In fact, the stepped-up strikes have coincided with a deterioration in the security situation in Pakistan."

In Pakistan, a war of machine assassins is visibly provoking terror (and terrorism), as well as anger and hatred among people who are by no means fundamentalists. It is part of a larger destabilization of the country.

To those who know their air power history, that shouldn't be so surprising. Air power has had a remarkably stellar record when it comes to causing death and destruction, but a remarkably poor one when it comes to

16

breaking the will of nations, peoples, or even modest-sized organizations. Our drone wars are destructive, but they are unlikely to achieve Washington's goals.

The Future Awaits Us

If you want to read the single most chilling line yet uttered about drone warfare American-style, it comes at the end of Christopher Drew's piece. He quotes Brookings Institution analyst Peter Singer saying of our Predators and Reapers: "[T]hese systems today are very much Model T Fords. These things will only get more advanced."

In other words, our drone wars are being fought with the airborne equivalent of cars with cranks, but the "race" to the horizon is already underway. Some Reapers now have a far more sophisticated sensor system with 12 cameras capable of filming a two-and-a-half mile round area from 12 different angles. That program has been dubbed "Gorgon Stare", but it doesn't compare to the future 92-camera Argus program whose initial development is being funded by the Pentagon's blue-skies outfit, the Defense Advanced Research Projects Agency.

Soon enough, a single pilot may be capable of handling not one but perhaps three drones, and drone armaments will undoubtedly grow progressively more powerful and "precise." In the meantime, BAE Systems already has spent years developing the Taranis, a drone that should someday be "completely autonomous";

that is, it theoretically will do without human pilots.

By 2020, so claim UAV enthusiasts, drones could be engaging in aerial battle and choosing their victims themselves. As Robert S. Boyd of McClatchy reported, "The Defense Department is financing studies of autonomous, or self-governing, armed robots that could find and destroy targets on their own. On-board computer programs, not flesh-and-blood people, would decide whether to fire their weapons."

It's a particular sadness of our world that, in Washington, only the military can dream about the future in this way, and then fund the "arms race" of 2018 or 2035. Rest assured that no one with a governmental red cent is researching the healthcare system of 2018 or 2035, or the public education system of those years.

In the meantime, the skies of our world are filling with round-the-clock assassins. They will only evolve and proliferate. Of course, when we head to the movies, we like to identify with John Connor, the human resister, the good guy of this planet, against the evil machines. Elsewhere, however, as we fight our drone wars ever more openly, as we field mechanical techno-terminators with all-seeing eyes and loose our missiles from thousands of miles away ("*Hasta la Vista*, Baby!"), we undoubtedly look like something other than a nation of John Connors to those living under the Predators. It may not matter if the joysticks and consoles on those advanced machines are somewhat antiquated; to others, we are now the terminators of the planet, implacable machine assassins.

True, we can't send our drones into the past to wipe out the young Ayman al-Zawahiri in Cairo. True, the UAV enthusiasts, who are already imagining all-drone wars run by "ethical" machines, may never see anything like their fantasies come to pass. Still, the fact that without the help of a single advanced cyborg we are already in the process of creating a Terminator planet should give us pause for thought... or not.

An MQ-1 Predator unmanned aerial vehicle sits in a hangar at Balad Air Base, Iraq, waiting for its next mission. (U.S. Air Force photo/Airman 1st Class Jonathan Steffen)

Chapter 2

Droning On

Tom Engelhardt

For drone freaks (and these days Washington seems full of them), here's the good news: Drones are hot! Not long ago -- 2006 to be exact -- the Air Force could barely get a few armed unmanned aerial vehicles (UAVs) into the air at once; by late 2009, the number was 38; beyond that, in every sense, the sky's the limit.

Better yet, for the latest generation of armed surveillance drones -- the ones with the chill-you-to-your-bones sci-fi names of Predators and Reapers (as in Grim) -- whole new surveillance capabilities will soon be available. Their newest video system has been dubbed Gorgon Stare after the creature in Greek mythology whose gaze turned its victims to stone.

What we're talking about here is the gaze of the gods, updated in corporate labs for the modern American war-fighter -- a gaze that can be focused on whatever runs, walks, crawls, or creeps just about anywhere on the planet 24/7, with an instant ability to blow it away. And what's true of video capacity will be no less true of the next generation of drone sensors -- and, of course, of drone weaponry like that "5-pound missile the size of a loaf of French bread" meant in some near-robotic future to replace the present 100-pound Hellfire missile, possibly on the Avenger or Predator C, the next generation drone under development at General Atomics Aeronautical Systems. Everything, in fact, will be almost infinitely upgradeable, since we're still in the robotics equivalent of the age of the "horseless carriage," as Peter Singer of the Brookings Institution assures us. (Just hold your hats, for instance, when the first nano-drones make it onto the scene! They will, according to Jane Mayer of the *New Yorker*, be able to "fly after their prey like a killer bee through an open window.")

Not only that, but drones are leaving the air for the high seas where they are called unmanned surface vehicles (USVs). In fact, Israel -- along with the U.S. leading the way on drones -- has launched the first of its USVs off the coast of Hamas-controlled Gaza. The U.S. can't be far behind and it seems that, like their airborne cousins, these ships, too, will be weaponized.

Taking the Measure of a Slam-Dunk Weapons System

Robot war. It just couldn't be cooler, could it? Especially if the only blood you spill is the other guy's, since our "pilots" are flying those planes from thousands of miles away. Soon, it seems, the world will be a drone fest. In his first nine months in office, President Obama authorized more drone attacks in the Pakistani tribal borderlands than the Bush administration had in its last three years.

In Washington, drones are even considered the "de-escalatory" option for the Afghan War by some critics, while former CIA Director Leon Panetta, whose agency ran our drone war in Pakistan, hailed them as "the only game in town in terms of confronting or trying to disrupt the al-Qaeda leadership." Among the few people who haven't adored them here were the hard-core war-fighters who didn't want an armada of robot planes standing in the way of sending in oodles more troops. The vice president, however, has proved a drone-atic. He loves 'em to death and reportedly has long wanted to up their missions, especially in Pakistan, rather than go the oodles route.

Obama's first secretary of defense Robert Gates jumped onto the drone bandwagon early. He had long pressed the Air Force to invest ever less in expensive manned aircraft -- he called the F-35, still in development, the last manned fighter aircraft -- and ever more in the robotic kind. After all, they're so lean, mean, and high-tech sexy -- for *Newsweek*, they fall into the category of "weapons porn" -- that what's not to like?

Okay, maybe there's the odd scrooge around like Philip Alston, the U.N. special rapporteur on extrajudicial executions, who complained to the press that the U.S. program might involve war crimes under international law: "We need the United States to be more up front and say,

'OK, we're willing to discuss some aspects of this program,' otherwise you have the really problematic bottom line that the CIA is running a program that is killing significant numbers of people and there is absolutely no accountability in terms of the relevant international laws."

But somebody's always going to be a nay-sayer. And let's face it, just about everyone who matters to the mainstream media swears that drones are much more "precise" in their "extrajudicial executions" than traditional air methods, which can be so messy. Better yet, when nothing in Afghanistan or Pakistan seems to be working out, the drones are actually doing the job. They've been reportedly knocking off the bad guys right and left. At least 13 senior al-Qaeda leaders and one senior Taliban leader (aka "high-value targets") had been killed by the drones by the end of 2009, according to the *Long War Journal*, and many more "foot soldiers" had been taken out as well.

And they're not just the obvious slam-dunk weapons system for our present problems in Afghanistan and Pakistan. They're potentially the royal path to the future when it comes to war-fighting, which is surely something else to be excited about.

The Wonder Weapons Succeed -- at Home

So why am I not excited -- other than the fact that the drones are also killing civilians in disputed but significant numbers in the Pakistani tribal borderlands, creating enemies and animosity wherever they strike, and turning us into a nation of 24/7 assassins beyond the law or accountability of any sort? Thought of another way, the drones put wings on the original Bush-era Guantanamo principle -- that Americans have the inalienable right to act as global judge, jury, and executioner, and when doing so are beyond the reach of any court or law.

And here's another factor that dulls my excitement just a tad -- if the history of air warfare has shown one thing, it's this: it never breaks populations. Rather, it only increases their sense of unity, as in London during the Blitz under Winston Churchill, in Germany under Adolf Hitler, Imperial Japan under Emperor Hirohito, North Korea under Kim Il Sung, North Vietnam under Ho Chi Minh, and of course (though we never put ourselves in such company, being the exceptions to all history), the United States after 9/11 under George W. Bush. Why should the peoples of rural Afghanistan and the Pakistani borderlands be any different?

Oh, and there's just one more reason that comes to mind: it so happens that I can see the future when it comes to drones, and it's dismal. I'm no prophet -- it's only that I've already lived through so much of that future. In fact, we all have.

Militarily speaking, we might as well be in the film *Groundhog Day* in which Bill Murray and Andie MacDowell are forced to live out the same 24 hours again and again -- with all the grimness of that idea and none of the charm of those actors. In my lifetime, I've repeatedly seen advanced weapons systems or mind-boggling technologies of war hailed as near-utopian paths to victory and future peace (just as the atomic bomb was soon after my birth). In the Vietnam War, the glories of "the electronic battlefield" were limned as an antidote to brute and ineffective American air power. That high-tech, advanced battlefield of invisible sensors was to bring an end to the impunity of guerrillas and infiltrating enemy armies. No longer capable of going anywhere undetected, they would have nowhere to hide.

In the 1980s, it was President Ronald Reagan's Strategic Defense Initiative, quickly dubbed "Star Wars" by its critics, a label that he accepted with amusement. ("If you will pardon my stealing a film line -- the Force is with us," he said in his usual genial way.) His dream, as he told the American people, was to create an "impermeable" anti-missile shield over the United States -- "like a roof protects a family from rain" -- that would end the possibility of nuclear attack from the Soviet Union and so create peace in our time (or, if you were of a more cynical turn of mind, the possibility of a freebie nuclear assault on the Soviets).

In the Gulf War, "smart bombs" and smart missiles were praised as the military saviors of the moment. They were to give war the kind of precision that would lower civilian deaths to the vanishing point and, as the neocons of the Bush administration would claim in the next decade, free the U.S. military to "decapitate" any regime we loathed. All this would be possible without so much as touching the civilian population (which would, of course, then welcome us as liberators). And later, there was "netcentric warfare," that Rumsfeldian high-tech favorite. Its promise was that advanced information-sharing technology would turn a Military Lite into an uplinked force so savvy about changing battlefield realities and so crushing that a mere demo or two would cow any "rogue" nation or insurgency into submission.

Of course, you know the results of this sort of magical thinking about wonder weapons (or technologies) and their properties just as well as I do. The atomic bomb ended nothing, but led to an almost half-century-long nuclear superpower standoff/nightmare, as well as to nuclear proliferation, and so to the possibility that, someday, even terrorists might possess such weapons. The electronic battlefield was incapable of staving off defeat in Vietnam. That impermeable anti-missile shield never came even faintly close to making it into our skies. Those "smart bombs" of the Gulf War proved remarkably dumb, while the 50 "decapitation" strikes the Bush administration launched against Saddam Hussein's regime on the first day of the 2003 invasion of Iraq took out not a single Iraqi leader, but "dozens" of civilians. And the history of the netcentric military in Iraq is well known. Its "success" sent Secretary of Defense Rumsfeld into retirement and ignominy.

In the same way, robot drones as assassination weapons will prove to be just another weapons system rather than a panacea for American warriors. To date, in fact, there is at least as much evidence in Pakistan and Afghanistan that the drones are helping to spread war as that they are staunching it.

Yet, the above summary is, at best, only half the story. None of these wonder weapons or technologies succeeded in their moment, or as advertised, but that fact stopped none of them from embedding themselves in our American world. From the atomic bomb came a whole nuclear landscape that included the Strategic Air Command, weapons labs, production plants, missile silos, corporate interests, and an enormous world-destroying arsenal (as well as proliferating versions of the same, large and small, across the planet). Nor did the electronic battlefield go away. Quite the opposite -- it came home and entered our everyday world in the form of sensors, cameras, surveillance equipment and the like, now implanted from our borders to our cities.

True, Reagan's impermeable shield was the purest of nuclear fantasies, but the "high frontiersmen" gathered and, taking a sizeable bite of the military budget, went on a decades-long binge of way-out research, space warfare plans and boondoggles of all sorts, including the staggeringly expensive, still not operational anti-missile system that the Bush and now Obama administrations have struggled to emplace somewhere in Europe. Similarly, ever newer generations of smart bombs and ever brighter missiles have been, and are being, developed *ad infinitum.*

Rarely do wonder weapons or wonder technologies disappoint enough to disappear. Each of these is, in fact, now surrounded by its own mini-version of the military-industrial complex, with its own set of corporate players, special lobbyists in Washington, specific interests, and congressional boosters. Each has installed a typical revolving door that the relevant Pentagon officials and officers can spin through once their military careers are over. This is no less true for that wonder weapon of our moment, the robot drone. In fact, you can already see the military-industrial-drone-robotics complex in formation. Take just one figure, Tony Tether, who for seven years was the head of the Defense Advanced Research Projects Agency (DARPA), which did its share of advanced robotics research. When he left the Pentagon, it was, according to Noah Shachtman, who runs *Wired's* Danger Room blog, to join "an advisory panel of Scientific Systems Company, Inc., which works on robotics projects for the Pentagon. Shortly thereafter, he joined the board of Aurora Flight

Sciences, Inc., developers of military unmanned aircraft." He also became "a part-time technical consultant and 'strategic advisor' for the influencers at The Livingston Group" which represents some large defense contractors like Northrop Grumman and Raytheon.

The drone industry, too, already has its own congressional representatives and "caucus." Republican Congressman Duncan Hunter, for instance, is a major drone booster. In April 2009, he insisted that "we must also press forward with the development of the next generation of UAVs, including the Predator C. During my service in the Marine Corps, I engaged targets with the Predator A and B Series, and I recognize the advantages offered by Predator C." In 2008, General Atomics, whose "affiliate" makes the Predator drone, gave $6,000 to Hunter's election campaign committee, making it his 13th largest contributor. That company was also the number two contributor to his Peace Through Strength political action committee.

In the American Grain

This, then, is the future that you can see just as well as I can. As the Obama administration upped the ante on drone use in Pakistan and Afghanistan, it ensured not the end of al-Qaeda or the Taliban, but the long life of robot war within our ever more militarized society. And by the time this set of robotic dreams fails to pan out, it won't matter. Yet another mini-sector of the military-industrial complex will be etched into the American grain.

Whatever the short-term gains from introducing drone warfare in these last years, we are now locked into the 24/7 assassination trade -- with our own set of non-suicide bombers on the job into eternity. This may pass for sanity in Washington, but it's surely helping to pave the road to hell.

Haven't any of these folks ever seen a sci-fi film? Are none of them *Terminator* fans? Are they sure they want to open the way to unlimited robot war, keeping in mind that, if this is the latest game in town, it won't remain mainly an American one for long. And just wait until the first Iranian drone takes out the first Baluchi guerrilla supported by American funds somewhere in Pakistan. Then let's see just what we think about the right of any nation to summarily execute its enemies -- and anyone else in the vicinity -- by drone.

Is this actually what we Americans want to be known for? And if we let this happen, and General Atomics is working double or triple shifts to turn out ever more, ever newer generations of robot warriors, while the nation suffers persistently high levels of unemployment, who exactly will think about shutting them down?

A flightline ground crew secures the Global Hawk unmanned aircraft system for towing to a secure hangar at Andersen Air Force Base, Guam. The UAS has a wing span of 116 feet and is designed to cruise at extremely high altitudes. (U.S. Air Force photo/Senior Airman Miranda Moorer)

Chapter 3

The Forty-Year Drone War

Nick Turse

One moment there was the hum of a motor in the sky above. The next, on a morning in Afghanistan's Helmand province, a missile blasted a home, killing 13 people. Days later, the same increasingly familiar mechanical whine preceded two missiles that slammed into a compound in Degan village in the tribal North Waziristan district of Pakistan, killing three.

What were once unacknowledged, relatively infrequent targeted killings of suspected militants or terrorists in the Bush years have become commonplace under the Obama administration. And following a devastating December 30, 2009 suicide attack by a Jordanian double agent on a CIA forward operating base in Afghanistan, unmanned aerial drones began hunting humans in the Af-Pak war zone at a record pace. In Pakistan, an "unprecedented number" of strikes -- which have killed armed guerrillas and civilians alike -- have led to more fear, anger, and outrage in the tribal areas, as the CIA, with help from the U.S. Air Force, wages the most public "secret" war of modern times.

In neighboring Afghanistan, unmanned aircraft, for years in short supply and tasked primarily with surveillance missions, have increasingly been used to assassinate suspected militants as part of an aerial surge that significantly outpaced the highly publicized "surge" of ground forces President Obama approved as 2009 ended. And yet, unprecedented as it may be in size and scope, the present ramping up of the drone war is only the opening salvo in a planned 40-year Pentagon surge to create fleets of ultra-advanced, heavily-armed, increasingly autonomous, all-seeing, hypersonic unmanned aerial systems (UAS).

Today's Surge

Drones are the hot weapons of the moment and the Quadrennial Defense Review of 2010 -- a four-year outline of Department of Defense strategies, capabilities, and priorities to fight current wars and counter future threats -- reflected this focus. As the *Washington Post* reported, "The pilotless drones used for surveillance and attack missions in Afghanistan and Pakistan are a priority, with the goals of speeding up the purchase of new Reaper drones and expanding Predator and Reaper drone flights through 2013."

The MQ-1 Predator -- first used in Bosnia and Kosovo in the 1990s -- and its newer, larger, and deadlier progeny, the MQ-9 Reaper, have been firing missiles and dropping bombs at an unprecedented pace. In 2008, there were reportedly between 27 and 36 U.S. drone attacks as part of the CIA's covert war in Pakistan. In 2009, there were 45 to 53 such strikes. In just the first 18 days of January 2010, there were 11 of them.

Meanwhile, in Afghanistan, as the U.S. Air Force instituted a much-publicized decrease in piloted air strikes to cut down on civilian casualties, UAS attacks increased to record levels.

The Air Force has created an interconnected global command-and-control system to carry out its robot war in Afghanistan (and as Noah Shachtman of *Wired's* Danger Room blog has reported, to assist the CIA in its drone strikes in Pakistan as well). Evidence of this can be found at high-tech U.S. bases around the world where drone pilots and other personnel control the planes themselves and the data streaming back from them. These sites include a converted medical warehouse at Al-Udeid Air Base, a billion-dollar facility in the Persian Gulf nation of Qatar where the Air Force secretly oversees its on-going drone wars; Kandahar and Jalalabad Air Fields in Afghanistan, where the drones are physically based; the global operations center at Nevada's Creech Air Base, where the Air Force's "pilots" fly drones by remote control from thousands of miles away; and -- perhaps most importantly -- at Wright-Patterson Air Force Base, a 12-square-mile facility in Dayton, Ohio, named after the two local brothers who invented powered flight in 1903. This is where the bills for the current drone surge -- as well as limited numbers of strikes in Yemen, Somalia, and elsewhere -- come due and are, quite literally, paid.

In the waning days of December 2009, in fact, the Pentagon cut two sizeable checks to ensure that unmanned operations involving the MQ-1 Predator and the MQ-9 Reaper would continue full-speed ahead into the future. The 703rd Aeronautical Systems Squadron based at Wright-Patterson signed a $38 million contract with defense giant Raytheon for logistics support for the targeting systems of both drones. At the same time, the squadron inked a deal worth $266 million with mega-defense contractor General Atomics, which makes the Predator and Reaper drones, to provide management services, logistics support, repairs, software maintenance, and other functions for both drone programs. These deals essentially ensured that, in the years ahead, the stunning increase in drone operations would continue.

The contracts, however, were only initial down payments on an enduring drone surge designed to carry U.S. unmanned aerial operations forward, ultimately for decades.

Drone Surge: The Longer View

Back in 2004, the Air Force could put a total of only five drone combat air patrols (CAPs) -- each consisting of four air vehicles -- in the skies over American war zones at any one time. By 2009, that number was 38, a 660% increase according to the Air Force. Similarly, between 2001 and 2008, hours of surveillance coverage for U.S. Central Command, encompassing both the Iraqi and Afghan war zones, as well as Pakistan and Yemen, showed a massive spike of 1,431%.

In the meantime, flight hours went through the roof. In 2004, for example, Reapers, just beginning to soar, flew 71 hours in total, according to Air Force documents; in 2006, that number had risen to 3,123 hours; in 2009, 25,391 hours. In 2010, the Air Force projected that the combined flight hours of all its drones -- Predators, Reapers, and unarmed RQ-4 Global Hawks -- would exceed 250,000 hours, about the total number of hours flown by all Air Force drones from 1995-2007.

More flight time will, undoubtedly, mean more killing. According to Peter Bergen and Katherine Tiedemann of the Washington-based think tank the New America Foundation, in the Bush years, from 2006 into 2009, there were 41 drone strikes in Pakistan, which killed 454 militants and civilians. In 2009, under the Obama administration, there were 42 strikes that left 453 people dead. A report by the Pakistan Institute for Peace Studies, an Islamabad-based independent research organization that tracks security issues, claimed an even larger number, 667 people -- most of them civilians -- killed by U.S. drone strikes that year.

While assisting the CIA's drone operations in the Pakistani tribal borderlands, the Air Force has been increasing its own unmanned aerial hunter-killer missions. In 2007 and 2008, for example, Air Force Predators and Reapers fired missiles during 244 missions in Iraq and Afghanistan. In fact, while all the U.S. armed services have pursued unmanned aerial warfare, the Air Force has outpaced each of them.

From 2001, when armed drone operations began, until the spring of 2009, the Air Force fired 703 Hellfire missiles and dropped 132 GBU-12s (500-pound laser-guided bombs) in combat operations. The Army, by comparison, launched just two Hellfire missiles and two smaller GBU-44 Viper Strike munitions in the same time period. The disparity should only grow, since the Army's drones remain predominantly small surveillance aircraft, while in 2009 the Air Force shifted all outstanding orders for the medium-sized Predator to the even more formidable Reaper, which is not only twice as fast but has 600% more payload capacity, meaning a larger capacity for bombs and missiles.

In addition, the more heavily armed Reapers, which can now loiter over an area for 10 to 14 hours without refueling, will be able to spot and track ever more targets via an increasingly sophisticated video monitoring system. According to Air Force Lt. Gen. David Deptula, then the Deputy Chief of Staff for Intelligence, Surveillance, and Reconnaissance, the first three "Gorgon Stare pods" -- new wide-area sensors that provide surveillance capabilities over large swathes of territory -- would be installed on Reapers operating in Afghanistan in the spring of 2010.

A technology not available for the older Predator, Gorgon Stare will allow a pilot back at a distant base to stare at a tiled screen with a composite picture of the streaming battlefield video, even as field commanders analyze a portion of the digital picture, panning, zooming, and tilting the image to meet their needs.

A more advanced set of "pods" will allow 30 operators to view 30 video images simultaneously. In other words, via video feeds from a single Reaper drone, operators could theoretically track 30 different people heading in 30 directions from a single Afghan compound. The following generation of sensors promises 65 such feeds, according to Air Force documents, a more than 6,000% increase in effectiveness over the Predator's video system. The Air Force is, however, already overwhelmed just by drone video currently being sent back from the war zones and, in the years ahead, risks "drowning in data," according to Deptula.

The 40-Year Plan

While, like the Army, the Navy is working on its own future drone warfare capacity -- in the air as well as on and even under the water -- the Air Force is involved in striking levels of futuristic planning for robotic war. It envisions a future previously imagined only in sci-fi movies like the *Terminator* series.

As a start, the Defense Advanced Research Projects Agency is already looking into radically improving on Gorgon Stare with an "Autonomous Real-time Ground Ubiquitous Surveillance-Infrared (ARGUS-IR) System." In the obtuse language of military research and development, it will, according to DARPA, provide a "real-time, high-resolution, wide area video persistent surveillance capability that allows joint forces to keep critical areas of interest under constant surveillance with a high degree of target location accuracy" via as many as "130 'Predator-like' steerable video streams to enable real-time tracking and monitoring and enhanced situational awareness during evening hours."

In translation, that means the Air Force will quite literally be flooded with video information from future battlefields; and every "advance" of this sort means bulking up the global network of facilities, systems, and personnel capable of receiving, monitoring, and interpreting the data streaming in from distant digital eyes. All of it, of course, is specifically geared toward "target location," that is, pinpointing people on one side of the world so that Americans on the other side can watch, track, and in many cases, kill them.

In addition to enhanced sensors and systems like ARGUS-IR, the Air Force has a long-term vision for drone warfare that is barely beginning to be realized. Predators and Reapers have already been joined in Afghanistan by a newer, formerly secret drone, a "low observable unmanned aircraft system" first spotted in 2007 and dubbed the "Beast of Kandahar" before observers were sure what it actually was. It is now known to be a Lockheed Martin-manufactured unmanned aerial vehicle, the RQ-170 -- a drone which the Air Force blandly notes was designed to "directly support combatant commander needs for intelligence, surveillance and reconnaissance to locate targets." According to military sources, the sleek, stealthy surveillance craft has been designated to replace the antique Lockheed U-2 spy plane, which has been in use since the 1950s.

In the coming years, the RQ-170 is slated to be joined in the skies of America's "next wars" by a fleet of drones with ever newer, more sophisticated capabilities and destructive powers. Looking into the future, Deptula said the most essential need, according to an *Aviation Week* report, was "long-range [reconnaissance and] precision strike" -- that is, more eyes in far off skies and more lethality. He added, "We cannot move into a future without a platform that allows [us] to project power long distances and to meet advanced threats in a fashion that gives us an advantage that no other nation has."

This means bigger, badder, faster drones -- armed to the teeth -- with sensor systems to monitor wide swathes of territory and the ability to loiter overhead for days on end waiting for human targets to appear and, in due course, be vaporized by lethal munitions. It's a future built upon advanced technologies designed to make targeted killings -- remote-controlled assassinations -- ever more effortless.

Over the horizon and deep into what was, until recently, only a silver-screen fantasy, the Air Force envisions a wide array of unmanned aircraft, from tiny insect-like robots to enormous "tanker size" pilotless planes. According to the *United States Air Force Unmanned Aircraft Systems Flight Plan 2009-2047*, each will be slated to take over specific war-making functions. Those nano-sized drones, for instance, are set to specialize in indoor reconnaissance -- they're small enough to fly through windows or down ventilation shafts -- and carry out lethal attacks, undertake computer-disabling cyber-attacks, and swarm, as would a group of angry bees, of their own volition. Slightly larger micro-sized Small Tactical Unmanned Aircraft Systems (STUAS) are supposed to act as "transformers" -- altering their form to allow for flying, crawling and non-visual sensing capabilities. They might fill sentry, counter-drone, surveillance, and lethal attack roles.

Additionally, the Air Force envisions small and medium "fighter sized" drones with lethal combat capabilities that would put the current UAS air fleet to shame. Today's medium-sized Reapers are set to be replaced by next generation MQ-Ma drones that will be "networked, capable of partial autonomy, all-weather and modular with capabilities supporting electronic warfare (EW), CAS [close air support], strike and multi-INT [multiple intelligence] ISR [intelligence, surveillance and reconnaissance] missions' platform."

The language may not be elegant, much less comprehensible, but if these future fighter aircraft actually come online they will not only send today's remaining Top Gun pilots to the showers, but may even sideline tomorrow's drone human operators, who, if all goes as planned, will have ever fewer duties. Unlike today's drones, which must take off and land with human guidance, the MQ-Ma's will be automated and drone operators will simply be there to monitor the aircraft.

Next up will be the MQ-Mb, theoretically capable of taking over even more roles once assigned to traditional fighter-bombers and spy planes, including the suppression of enemy air defenses, bombing and strafing of ground targets, and surveillance missions. These will also be designed to fly more autonomously and be better linked-in to other drone "platforms" for cooperative missions involving many aircraft under the command of a single "pilot." Imagine, for instance, one operator overseeing a single command drone that holds sway over a small squadron of autonomous drones carrying out a coordinated air attack on clusters of people in some far off land, incinerating them in small groups across a village, town or city.

Finally, perhaps 30 to 40 years from now, the MQ-Mc drone would incorporate all of the advances of the MQ-M line, while being capable of everything from dog-fighting to missile defense. With such new technology will, of course, come new policies and new doctrines. In the years ahead, the Air Force intends to make drone-related policy decisions on everything from treaty obligations to automatic target engagement -- robotic killing without a human in the loop. The latter extremely controversial development is already envisioned as a possible post-2025 reality.

2047: What's Old is New Again

The year 2047 is the target date for the Air Force's Holy Grail, the capstone for its long-term plan to turn the skies over to war-fighting drones. In 2047, the Air Force intends to rule the skies with MQ-Mc drones and "special" super-fast, hypersonic drones for which neither viable technology nor any enemies with any comparable programs or capabilities yet exist. Despite this, the Air Force is intent on making these super-fast hunter-killer systems a reality by 2047. "Propulsion technology and materials that can withstand the extreme heat will likely take 20 years to develop. This technology will be the next generation air game-changer. Therefore the prioritization of the funding for the specific technology development should not wait until the emergence of a critical COCOM [combatant command] need," says the Air Force's 2009-2047 UAS "Flight Plan."

If anything close to the Air Force's dreams comes to fruition, the "game" will indeed be radically changed. By 2047, there's no telling how many drones will be circling over how many heads in how many places across the planet. There's no telling how many millions or billions of flight hours will have been flown, or how many people, in how many countries will have been killed by remote-controlled, bomb-dropping, missile-firing, judge-jury-and-executioner drone systems.

There's only one given. If the U.S. still exists in its present form, is still solvent, and still has a functioning Pentagon of the present sort, a new plan will already be well underway to create the war-making technologies of 2087. By then, in ever more places, people will be living with the sort of drone war that now worries only those in places like Degan village. Ever more people will know that unmanned aerial systems packed with missiles and bombs are loitering in their skies. By then, there undoubtedly won't even be that lawnmower-engine sound indicating that a missile may soon plow into your neighbor's home.

For the Air Force, such a prospect is the stuff of dreams, a bright future for unmanned, hypersonic lethality; for the rest of the planet, it's a potential nightmare from which there may be no waking.

An Air Force MQ-9 Reaper unmanned aerial attack vehicle prepares to land after a mission in Afghanistan. (U.S. Air Force Photo/Staff Sgt. Brian Ferguson)

Chapter 4

The Perfect American Weapon

Tom Engelhardt

Admittedly, before George W. Bush had his fever dream, the U.S. had already put its first unmanned aerial vehicles (UAVs) or drone surveillance planes in the skies over Kosovo in the late 1990s. By November 2001, it had armed them with missiles and was flying them over Afghanistan.

In November 2002, a Predator drone would loose a Hellfire missile on a car in Yemen, a country with which we weren't at war. Six suspected al-Qaeda members, including a suspect in the bombing of the destroyer the USS *Cole* would be turned into twisted metal and ash in one of the first "targeted killings" of the American robotic era.

Just two months earlier, in September 2002, as the Bush administration was "introducing" its campaign to sell an invasion of Iraq to Congress and the American people, CIA Director George Tenet and Vice President Dick Cheney "trooped up to Capitol Hill" to brief four top Senate and House leaders on a hair-raising threat to the country. A "smoking gun" had been uncovered.

According to "new intelligence," Iraqi dictator Saddam Hussein had in his possession unmanned aerial vehicles advanced enough to be armed with biological and chemical weaponry. Worse yet, these were capable -- so the CIA director and vice president claimed -- of spraying that weaponry of mass destruction over cities on the east coast of the United States. It was just the sort of evil plan you might have expected from a man regularly compared to Adolf Hitler in our media, and the news evidently made an impression in Congress.

Democratic Senator Bill Nelson of Florida, for example, said that he voted for the administration's resolution authorizing force in Iraq because "I was told not only that [Saddam had weapons of mass destruction] and that he had the means to deliver them through unmanned aerial vehicles, but that he had the capability of transporting those UAVs outside of Iraq and threatening the homeland here in America, specifically by putting them on ships off the eastern seaboard."

In a speech in October 2002, President Bush then offered a version of this apocalyptic nightmare to the American public. Of course, like Saddam's supposed ability to produce "mushroom clouds" over American cities, the Iraqi autocrat's advanced UAVs (along with the ships needed to position them off the U.S. coast) were a feverish fantasy of the Bush era and would soon enough be forgotten. Instead, in the years to come, it would be American pilotless drones that would repeatedly attack

Iraqi urban areas with Hellfire missiles and bombs.

In those years, our drones would also strike repeatedly in Afghanistan, and especially in the tribal borderlands of Pakistan, where in an escalating "secret" or "covert" war, which has been no secret to anyone, multiple drone attacks often occur weekly. They are now considered so much the norm that, with humdrum headlines slapped on ("U.S. missile strike kills 12 in NW Pakistan"), they barely make it out of summary articles about war developments in the American press.

And yet those robotic planes, with their young "pilots" (as well as the camera operators and intelligence analysts who make up a drone "crew") sitting in front of consoles 7,000 miles away from where their missiles and bombs are landing, have become another kind of American fever dream. The drone is our latest wonder weapon and a bragging point in a set of wars where there has been little enough to brag about.

Former CIA director and now Secretary of Defense Leon Panetta has, for instance, called the Agency's drones flying over Pakistan "the only game in town" when it comes to destroying al-Qaeda; a typically anonymous U.S. official in a *Washington Post* report claimed of drone missile attacks, "We're talking about precision unsurpassed in the history of warfare"; or as Gordon Johnson of the Pentagon's Joint Forces Command told author

Peter Singer, speaking of the glories of drones: "They don't get hungry. They are not afraid. They don't forget their orders. They don't care if the guy next to them has been shot. Will they do a better job than humans? Yes."

Seven thousand of them, the vast majority surveillance varieties, are reportedly already being operated by the military, and that's before swarms of "mini-drones" come on line. Our American world is being redefined accordingly.

In February 2010, Greg Jaffe of the *Washington Post* caught something of this process when he spent time with Colonel Eric Mathewson, perhaps the most experienced Air Force officer in drone operations and on the verge of retirement. Mathewson, reported Jaffe, was trying to come up with an appropriately new definition of battlefield "valor" -- a necessity for most combat award citations -- to fit our latest corps of pilots at their video consoles. "Valor to me is not risking your life," the colonel told the reporter. "Valor is doing what is right. Valor is about your motivations and the ends that you seek. It is doing what is right for the right reasons. That to me is valor."

Smoking Drones

These days, CIA and administration officials troop up to Capitol Hill to offer briefings to Congress on the miraculous value of pilotless drones: in disrupting al-Qaeda, destroying its leadership or driving it "deeper into hiding," and taking out key figures in the Taliban. Indeed, what started as a 24/7 assassination campaign against al-Qaeda's top leadership has already widened considerably. The "target set" has by now reportedly expanded to take in ever lower-level militants in the tribal borderlands. In other words, a drone assassination campaign has morphed into the first full-scale drone war (and, as in all wars from the air, civilians are dying in unknown numbers).

If the temperature is again rising in Washington when it comes to these weapons, this time it's a fever of enthusiasm for the spectacular future of drones, of a time when single pilots should be able to handle multiple drones in operations in the skies over some embattled land, and of a far more distant moment when those drones should be able to handle themselves, flying, fighting, and making key decisions about just who to take out without a human being having to intervene.

When *we* possess such weaponry, it turns out, there's nothing unnerving or disturbing, apocalyptic or dystopian about it. Today, in the American homeland, not a single smoking drone is in sight.

Now it's the United States whose UAVs are ever more powerfully weaponized. It's the U.S. which is developing a 22-ton tail-less drone 20 times larger than a Predator that can fly at Mach 7 and (theoretically) land on the pitching deck of an aircraft carrier. It's the Pentagon which is planning to increase the funding of drone development by 700% over the next decade.

Admittedly, there is a modest counter-narrative to all this enthusiasm for our robotic prowess, "precision," and "valor." It involves legal types like Philip Alston, the United Nations special representative on extrajudicial executions. In mid-2010, for instance, he issued a 29-page report criticizing Washington's "ever-expanding entitlement for itself to target individuals across the globe." Unless limits are put on such claims, and especially on the CIA's drone war over Pakistan, he suggested, soon enough a plethora of states will follow in America's footprints, attacking people in other lands "labeled as terrorists by one group or another."

Such mechanized, long-distance warfare, he also suggested, would breach what respect remains for the laws of war. "Because operators are based thousands of miles away from the battlefield," he wrote, "and undertake operations entirely through computer screens and remote audio-feed, there is a risk of developing a 'PlayStation' mentality to killing."

Similarly, the ACLU filed a freedom of information lawsuit against the U.S. government, demanding that it "disclose the legal basis for its use of unmanned drones to conduct targeted killings overseas, as well as the ground rules regarding when, where, and against whom drone strikes can be authorized, and the number of civilian casualties they have caused."

But pay no mind to all this. The arguments may be legally compelling, but not in Washington, which has mounted a half-hearted claim of legitimate "self-defense," but senses that it's already well past the point where legalities matter. The die is cast, the money committed. The momentum for drone war and yet more drone war is overwhelming.

It's a done deal. Drone war is, and will be, us.

A Pilotless Military

If there are *zeitgeist* moments for products, movie stars, and even politicians, then such moments can exist for weaponry as well. The robotic drone is the Lady Gaga of this Pentagon moment.

It's a moment that could, of course, be presented as an apocalyptic nightmare in the style of the *Terminator* movies (with the U.S. as the soul-crushing Skynet), *or* as a remarkable tale of how "networking technology is expanding a home front that is increasingly relevant to day-to-day warfare" (as reporter Christopher Drew put it in the *New York Times*). It could be described as the arrival of a dystopian fantasy world of one-way slaughter verging on entertainment, *or* as the coming of a generation of homegrown video warriors who work "in camouflage uniforms, complete with combat boots, on open floors, with four computer monitors on each desk... and coffee and Red Bull help[ing] them get through the 12-hour shifts." It could be presented as the ultimate in cowardice -- the killing of people in a world you know nothing about from thousands of miles away -- *or* (as Col. Mathewson would prefer) a new form of valor.

The drones -- their use expanding exponentially, with ever newer generations on the drawing boards, and the planes even heading for "the homeland" -- could certainly be considered a demon spawn of modern warfare, *or* (as is generally the case in the U.S.) a remarkable example of American technological ingenuity, a problem-solver of the first order at a time when few American problems seem capable of solution. Thanks to our technological prowess, it's claimed that *we* can now kill *them*, wherever they may be lurking, at absolutely no cost to ourselves, other than the odd malfunctioning drone. Not that even all CIA operatives involved in the drone wars agree with that one. Some of them understand perfectly well that there's a price to be paid.

As it happens, the enthusiasm for drones is as much a fever dream as the one President Bush and his associates offered back in 2002, but it's also distinctly us. In fact, drone warfare fits America tighter than a glove. With its consoles, chat rooms, and first-person- shooter death machines, it certainly fits the skills of a generation raised on the computer, Facebook, and video games. That our valorous warriors, their day of battle done, can increasingly leave war behind and head home to the barbecue (or, given American life, the foreclosure) also fits an American mood of the moment.

The Air Force "detachments" that "manage" the drone war from places like Creech Air Force Base in Nevada are "detached" from war in a way that even an artillery unit significantly behind the battle lines or an American pilot in an F-16 over Afghanistan (who could, at least, experience engine failure) isn't. If the drone presents the most extreme version thus far of the detachment of human beings from the battlefield (on only one side, of course) and so launches a basic redefinition of what war is all about, it also catches something important about the American way of war.

After all, while this country garrisons the world, invests its wealth in its military, and fights unending, unwinnable frontier wars and skirmishes, most Americans are remarkably detached from all this. If anything, since Vietnam when an increasingly rebellious citizens' army proved disastrous for Washington's global aims, such detachment has been the goal of American war-making.

As a start, with no draft and so no citizen's army, war and the toll it takes is now the professional business of a tiny percentage of Americans (and their families). It occurs thousands of miles away and, in the Bush years, also became a heavily privatized, for-profit activity. As Pratap Chatterjee reported recently, "[E]very US soldier deployed to Afghanistan and Iraq is matched by at least one civilian working for a private company. All told, about 239,451 contractors work for the Pentagon in battle zones around the world." And a majority of those contractors aren't even U.S. citizens.

If drones have entered our world as media celebrities, they have done so largely without debate among that detached populace. In a sense, our wars abroad could be thought of as the equivalent of so many drones. We send our troops off, then go home for dinner and put them out of mind. The question is: Have we redefined our detachment as a new version of citizenly valor (and covered it over by a constant drumbeat of "support for our troops")?

Under these circumstances, it's hardly surprising that a "pilotless" force should, in turn, develop the sort of contempt for civilians that was on display during the 2010 flap over the derogatory comments of Afghan war commander General Stanley McChrystal and his aides about Obama administration officials.

The Globalization of Death

Maybe what we need is the return of George W. Bush's fever dream from the American oblivion in which it's now interred. He was beyond wrong, of course, when it came to Saddam Hussein and Iraqi drones, but he wasn't completely wrong about the dystopian Drone World to come. There are now reportedly more than 40 countries developing versions of those pilot-less planes. In 2010, the Iranians announced that they were starting up production lines for both armed and unarmed drones. Hezbollah used them against Israel in the 2006 summer war, years after Israel began pioneering their use in targeted killings of Palestinians.

Right now, in what still remains largely a post-Cold War arms race of one, the U.S. is racing to produce ever more advanced drones to fight our wars, with few competitors in sight. We're also obliterating classic ideas of national sovereignty, and of who can be killed by whom under what circumstances. In the process, we may not just be obliterating enemies, but creating them wherever our drones buzz overhead and our missiles strike.

We are also creating the (il)legal framework for future war on a frontier where we won't long be flying solo. And when the first Iranian, or Russian, or Chinese missile-armed drones start knocking off their chosen sets of "terrorists," we won't like it one bit. When the first "suicide drones" appear, we'll like it even less. And if drones with the ability to spray chemical or biological weapons finally do make the scene, we'll be truly unnerved.

In the 1990s, we were said to be in an era of "globalization" which was widely hailed as good news. Now, the U.S. and its detached populace are pioneering a new era of killing that respects no boundaries, relies on the self-definitions of whoever owns the nearest drone, and establishes planetary free-fire zones. It's a nasty combination, this globalization of death.

Airman 1st Class Troy Spence, a 62nd Expeditionary Reconnaissance Squadron crew chief, looks over technical data on his laptop while performing maintenance on an MQ-1 Predator at Bagram Air Base, Afghanistan. Airman Spence is deployed from the 432nd Aircraft Maintenance Squadron at Creech Air Force Base, Nev. (U.S. Air Force photo/Master Sgt. Demetrius Lester)

Chapter 5

Top Guns No More

Tom Engelhardt

When men initially made war in the air, the imagery that accompanied them was of knights jousting in the sky. Just check out movies like *Wings*, which won the first Oscar for Best Picture in 1927 (or any Peanuts cartoon in which Snoopy takes on the Red Baron in a literal "dogfight"). As late as 1986, five years after two American F-14s shot down two Soviet jets flown by Libyan pilots over the Mediterranean's Gulf of Sidra, it was still possible to make the movie *Top Gun*. In it, Tom Cruise played "Maverick," a U.S. Naval aviator triumphantly involved in a similar incident. (*He* shoots down three MiGs.)

Admittedly, by then American air-power films had long been in decline. In Vietnam, the U.S. had used its air superiority to devastating effect, bombing the north and blasting the south, but go to American Vietnam films and, while that U.S. patrol walks endlessly into a South Vietnamese village with mayhem to come, the air is largely devoid of planes.

Consider *Top Gun* an anomaly. Anyway, it's been 25 years since that film topped the box-office -- and don't hold your breath for a repeat at your local multiplex. After all, there's nothing left to base such a film on.

To put it simply, it's time for Americans to take the "war" out of "air war." These days, we need a new set of terms to explain what U.S. air power actually does.

Start this way: American "air superiority" in any war the U.S. now fights is total. In fact, the last time American jets met enemy planes of any sort in any skies was in the First Gulf War in 1991, and since Saddam Hussein's once powerful air force didn't offer much opposition -- most of its planes fled to Iran -- that was brief. The last time U.S. pilots faced anything like a serious challenge in the skies was in North Vietnam in the early 1970s. Before that, you have to go back to the Korean War in the early 1950s.

This, in fact, is something American military types take great pride in. Addressing the cadets of the Air Force Academy in March 2011, for example, Secretary of Defense Robert Gates stated: "There hasn't been a U.S. Air Force airplane lost in air combat in nearly 40 years, or an American soldier attacked by enemy aircraft since Korea."

And he's probably right, though it's also possible that the last American plane shot down in aerial combat was U.S. Navy pilot Michael Scott Speicher's jet in the First Gulf War. (The Navy continues to claim that the plane was felled by a surface-to-air missile.) As an F-117A Stealth fighter was downed by a surface-to-air missile over Serbia in 1999, it's been more than 11 years since such a plane

61

was lost due to anything but mechanical malfunction. Yet in those years, the U.S. has remained almost continuously at war somewhere and has used air power extensively, as in its "shock and awe" launch to the invasion of Iraq, which was meant to "decapitate" Saddam Hussein and the rest of the Iraqi leadership. (No plane was lost, nor was an Iraqi leader of any sort taken out in those 50 decapitation attacks, but "dozens" of Iraqi civilians died.) You might even say that air power has continued to be the American way of war.

From a military point of view, this is something worth bragging about. It's just that the obvious conclusions are never drawn from it.

The Valor of Pilots

Let's begin with this: to be a "Top Gun" in the U.S. military today is to be in staggeringly less danger than any American who gets into a car and heads just about anywhere, given this country's annual toll of about 34,000 fatal car crashes. In addition, there is far less difference than you might imagine between piloting a drone aircraft from a base thousands of miles away and being inside the cockpit of a fighter jet.

Articles are now regularly written about drone aircraft "piloted" by teams sitting at consoles in places like Creech Air Force Base in Nevada. Meanwhile, their planes are loosing Hellfire missiles thousands of miles away in

Afghanistan (or, in the case of CIA "pilots," in the Pakistani tribal borderlands). Such news accounts often focus on the eerie safety of those pilots in "wartime" and their strange detachment from the actual dangers of war.

When it comes to pilots in actual planes flying over Afghanistan, we imagine something quite different -- and yet we shouldn't. Based on the record, those pilots might as well be in Nevada, since there is no enemy that can touch them. They are inviolate unless their own machines betray them and, with the rarest of imaginable exceptions, will remain so.

Nor does anyone here consider it an irony that the worst charge lodged by U.S. military spokespeople against their guerrilla enemies, whose recruits obviously can't take to the skies, is that they use "human shields" as a defense. This transgression against "the law of war" is typical of any outgunned guerrilla force which, in Mao Zedong's dictum, sees immense benefit in "swimming" in a "sea" of civilians. (If they didn't do so and fought like members of a regular army, they would, of course, be slaughtered.)

This is considered, however implicitly, a sign of ultimate cowardice. On the other hand, while a drone pilot cannot (yet) get a combat award citation for "valor," a jet fighter pilot can and no one -- here at least -- sees anything strange or cowardly about a form of warfare which guarantees the American side quite literal, godlike invulnerability.

War by its nature is often asymmetrical, as in the intervention by the U.S. and its allies in Libya in 2011, and sometimes hideously one-sided. The retreat that turns into a rout that turns into a slaughter is a relative commonplace of battle. But it cannot be war, as anyone has ever understood the word, if one side is *never* in danger. And yet that is American air war as it has developed since World War II.

It's a long path from knightly aerial jousting to air war as... well, what? We have no language for it, because accurate labels would prove deflating, pejorative, and exceedingly uncomfortable. You would perhaps need to speak of cadets at the Air Force Academy being prepared for "air slaughter" or "air assassination," depending on the circumstances.

From those cadets to a Secretary of Defense to reporters covering our wars, no one here is likely to accept the taking of "war" out of air war. And because of that, it is -- conveniently -- almost impossible for Americans to imagine how American-style war must seem to those in the lands where we fight.

Apologies All Around

Consider for a moment one form of war-related naming where our language changes all the time. That's the naming of our new generations of weaponry. In the case of those drones, the two main ones in U.S. battle zones at the moment are the Predator (as in the sci-fi film) and the Reaper (as in Grim). In both cases, the names imply an urge for slaughter and a sense of superiority verging on immortality.

And yet we don't take such names seriously. Though we've seen the movies (and most Afghans haven't), we don't imagine our form of warfare as like that of the Predator, that alien hunter of human prey, or a Terminator, that machine version of the same. If we did, we would have quite a different picture of ourselves, which would mean quite a different way of thinking about how we make war.

From the point of view of Afghans, Pakistanis, or other potential target peoples, those drones buzzing in the sky must seem very much like real-life versions of Predators or Terminators. They must, that is, seem alien and implacable like so many malign gods. After all, the weaponry from those planes is loosed without recourse; no one on the ground can do a thing to prevent it and little to defend themselves; and often enough the missiles and bombs kill the innocent along with those our warriors consider the guilty.

Take an event in early 2011 on a distant hillside in Afghanistan's Kunar Province where 10 boys, including two sets of brothers, were collecting wood for their families on a winter's day when the predators -- this time American helicopters evidently looking for insurgents who had rocketed a nearby American base --

arrived. Only one of the boys survived (with wounds) and he evidently described the experience as one of being "hunted" -- as the Predator hunts humans or human hunters stalk animals. They "hovered over us," he said, "scanned us, and we saw a green flash," then the helicopters rose and began firing.

For this particular nightmare, then-war commander General David Petraeus apologized directly to Afghan President Hamid Karzai, who has for years fruitlessly denounced U.S. and NATO air operations that have killed Afghan civilians. When an angered Karzai refused to accept his apology, then-Secretary of Defense Gates, on a surprise visit to the country, apologized as well, as did President Obama. And that was that -- for the Americans.

Forget for a moment what this incident tells us about a form of warfare in which helicopter pilots, reasonably close to the ground (and modestly more vulnerable than pilots in planes), can't tell boys with sticks from insurgents with weapons. The crucial thing to keep in mind is that, no matter how many apologies may be offered afterwards, this can't stop. According to the *Wall Street Journal*, death by helicopter in Afghanistan is, in fact, on the rise. It's in the nature of this kind of warfare. In fact, Afghan civilians have repeatedly, even repetitiously, been blown away from the air, with or without apologies, since 2001. Over these years, Afghan participants at wedding parties, funerals, and other rites have, for example, been wiped out with relative regularity, only sometimes with apologies to follow.

In the weeks that preceded the killing of those boys, for instance, a "NATO" -- these are usually American -- air attack took out four Afghan security guards protecting the work of a road construction firm and wounded a fifth, according to the police chief of Helmand Province; a similar "deeply regrettable incident" took out an Afghan army soldier, his wife, and his four children in Nangarhar Province; and a third, also in Kunar Province, wiped out 65 civilians, including women and children, according to Afghan government officials. Karzai recently visited a hospital and wept as he held a child wounded in the attack whose leg had been amputated.

The U.S. military did not weep. Instead, it rejected this claim of civilian deaths, insisting as it often does that the dead were "insurgents," and began -- as it typically does -- "investigating" the incident. General Petraeus managed to further offend Afghan officials when he visited the presidential palace in Kabul and reportedly claimed that some of the wounded children might have suffered burns not in an air attack but from their parents as punishment for bad behavior and were being counted in the casualty figures only to make them look worse.

Over the years, Afghan civilian casualties from the air have waxed and waned, depending on how much air power American commanders were willing to call in, but they have never ceased. As history tells us, air power and civilian deaths are inextricably bound together. They can't be separated, no matter how much anyone talks about "surgical" strikes and "precision" bombing. It's simply the barbaric essence, the very nature of this kind of war, to kill noncombatants.

One question sometimes raised about such casualties in Afghanistan is this: according to U.N. statistics, the Taliban (via roadside bombs and suicide bombers) kills far more civilians, including women and children, than do NATO forces, so why do the U.S.-caused deaths stick so in Afghan craws when we periodically investigate, apologize, and even pay survivors for their losses?

New York Times reporter Alissa J. Rubin puzzled over this and offered the following answer: "[T]hose that are caused by NATO troops appear to reverberate more deeply because of underlying animosity about foreigners in the country." This seems reasonable as far as it goes, but don't discount what air power adds to the foreignness of the situation.

Consider what the 20-year-old brother of two of the dead boys from the Kunar helicopter attack told the *Wall Street Journal* in a phone interview: "The only option I have is to pick up a Kalashnikov, RPG [rocket-propelled grenade], or a suicide vest to fight."

Whatever the Taliban may be, they remain part of Afghan society. They are there on the ground. They kill and they commit barbarities, but they suffer, too. In our version of air "war," however, the killing and the dying are perfectly and precisely, even surgically, separated. We kill, they die. It's that simple. Sometimes the ones we target to die do so; sometimes others stand in their stead. But no matter. We then deny, argue, investigate, apologize, and continue. We are, in that sense, implacable.

And one more thing: since we are incapable of thinking of ourselves as either predators or Predators, no less emotionless Terminators, it becomes impossible for us to see that our air "war" on terror is, in reality, a machine for creating what we then call "terrorists." It is part of an American Global War *for* Terror.

In other words, although air power has long been held up as part of the solution to terrorism, and though the American military now regularly boasts about the enemy body counts it produces, and the precision with which it does so, all of that, even when accurate, is also a kind of delusion -- and worse yet, one that transforms us into Predators and Terminators. It's not a pretty sight.

So count on this: there will be no more Top Guns. No knights of the air. No dogfights and sky-jousts. No valor. Just one-sided slaughter and targeted assassinations. That is where air power has ended up. Live with it.

Airmen assigned to the 432nd Aircraft Maintenance Squadron assemble an MQ-1 Predator. The six images on the side of the MQ-1 Predator symbolize the number of Hellfire missiles shot while in combat. (U.S. Air Force photo/Senior Airman Larry E. Reid Jr.)

Chapter 6

America's Secret Empire of Drone Bases

Nick Turse

They increasingly dot the planet. There's a facility outside Las Vegas where "pilots" work in climate-controlled trailers, another at a dusty camp in Africa formerly used by the French Foreign Legion, a third at a big air base in Afghanistan where Air Force personnel sit in front of multiple computer screens, and a fourth at an air base in the United Arab Emirates that almost no one talks about.

And that leaves at least 56 more such facilities to mention in an expanding American empire of drone bases being set up worldwide. Despite frequent news reports on the unmanned assassination campaigns launched in support of America's ever-widening undeclared wars and a spate of stories on drone bases in Africa and the Middle East, most of these facilities have remained unnoted, uncounted, and remarkably anonymous -- until now.

Run by the military, the Central Intelligence Agency, and their proxies, these bases -- some little more than desolate airstrips, others sophisticated command and control centers filled with computer screens and high-tech electronic equipment -- are the backbone of a new American robotic way of war. They are also the latest development in a long-evolving saga of American power projection abroad -- in this case, remote-controlled strikes anywhere on the planet with a minimal foreign "footprint" and little accountability.

Using military documents, press accounts, and other open source information, an in-depth analysis by TomDispatch has identified at least 60 bases integral to U.S. military and CIA drone operations. There may, however, be more, since a cloak of secrecy about drone warfare leaves the full size and scope of these bases distinctly in the shadows.

A Galaxy of Bases

Over the last decade, the American use of unmanned aerial vehicles (UAVs) and unmanned aerial systems (UAS) has expanded exponentially, as has media coverage of their use. On September 21, 2011, the *Wall Street Journal* reported that the military had deployed missile-armed MQ-9 Reaper drones on the "island nation of Seychelles to intensify attacks on al Qaeda affiliates, particularly in Somalia." A day earlier, a *Washington Post* piece also mentioned the same base on the tiny Indian Ocean archipelago, as well as one in the African nation of Djibouti, another under construction in Ethiopia, and a secret CIA airstrip being built for drones in an unnamed Middle Eastern country. (Some suspect it's Saudi Arabia.)

Post journalists Greg Miller and Craig Whitlock reported that the "Obama administration is assembling a constellation of secret drone bases for counterterrorism operations in the Horn of Africa and the Arabian Peninsula as part of a newly aggressive campaign to attack al-Qaeda affiliates in Somalia and Yemen." Within days, the *Post* also reported that a drone from the new CIA base in that unidentified Middle Eastern country had carried out the assassination of radical al-Qaeda preacher and American citizen Anwar al-Awlaki in Yemen.

With the killing of al-Awlaki, the Obama Administration has expanded its armed drone campaign to no fewer than six countries, though the CIA, which killed al-Awlaki, refuses to officially acknowledge its drone assassination program. The Air Force is less coy about its drone operations, yet there are many aspects of those, too, that remain in the shadows. Air Force spokesman Lieutenant Colonel John Haynes told TomDispatch that, "for operational security reasons, we do not discuss worldwide operating locations of Remotely Piloted Aircraft, to include numbers of locations around the world."

Still, those 60 military and CIA bases worldwide, directly connected to the drone program, tell us much about America's war-making future. From command and control and piloting to maintenance and arming, these facilities perform key functions that allow drone campaigns to continue expanding, as they have for more than a decade. Other bases are already under construction or in the planning stages. When presented with our list of Air Force sites within America's galaxy of drone bases, Lieutenant Colonel Haynes responded, "I have nothing further to add to what I've already said."

Even in the face of government secrecy, however, much can be discovered. Here, then, for the record is a TomDispatch accounting of America's drone bases in the United States and around the world.

The Near Abroad

News reports have frequently focused on Creech Air Force Base outside Las Vegas as ground zero in America's military drone campaign. Sitting in darkened, air-conditioned rooms 7,500 miles from Afghanistan, drone pilots dressed in flight suits remotely control MQ-9 Reapers and their progenitors, the less heavily-armed MQ-1 Predators. Beside them, sensor operators manipulate the TV camera, infrared camera, and other high-tech sensors on board the plane. Their faces are lit up by digital displays showing video feeds from the battle zone. By squeezing a trigger on a joystick, one of those Air Force "pilots" can unleash a Hellfire missile on a person half a world away.

While Creech gets the lion's share of media attention -- it even has its own drones on site -- numerous other bases on U.S. soil have played critical roles in America's drone wars. The same video-game-style warfare is carried out by U.S and British pilots not far away at Nevada's Nellis Air Force Base, the home of the Air Force's 2nd Special Operations Squadron (SOS). According to a factsheet provided to TomDispatch by the Air Force, the 2nd SOS and its drone operators are scheduled to be relocated to the Air Force Special Operations Command at Hurlburt Field in Florida sometime in early 2012.

Reapers or Predators are also being flown from Davis-Monthan Air Force Base in Arizona, Whiteman Air Force Base in Missouri, March Air Reserve Base in California, Springfield Air National Guard Base in Ohio, Cannon Air Force Base and Holloman Air Force Base in New Mexico, Ellington Airport in Houston, Texas, the Air National Guard base in Fargo, North Dakota, Ellsworth Air Force Base in South Dakota, and Hancock Field Air National Guard Base in Syracuse, New York. Reapers flown by Hancock's pilots are to begin taking off on training missions from the Army's Fort Drum, also in New York State.

Meanwhile, at Langley Air Force Base in Virginia, according to a report by the *New York Times*, teams of camouflage-clad Air Force analysts sit in a secret intelligence and surveillance installation monitoring cell-phone intercepts, high-altitude photographs, and most notably, multiple screens of streaming live video from drones in Afghanistan. They call it "Death TV" and are constantly instant-messaging with and talking to commanders on the ground in order to supply them with real-time intelligence on enemy troop movements. Air Force analysts also closely monitor the battlefield from Air Force Special Operations Command in Florida and a facility in Terre Haute, Indiana.

CIA drone operators also reportedly pilot their aircraft from the Agency's nearby Langley, Virginia headquarters. It was from there that analysts apparently watched footage of Osama bin Laden's compound in Pakistan, for example, thanks to video sent back by the RQ-170 Sentinel, the advanced drone nicknamed the "Beast of Kandahar." According to Air Force documents, the Sentinel is flown from both Creech Air Force Base and Tonopah Test Range in Nevada.

Predators, Reapers, and Sentinels are just part of the story. At Beale Air Force Base in California, Air Force personnel pilot the RQ-4 Global Hawk, an unmanned drone used for long-range, high-altitude surveillance missions, some of them originating from Anderson Air Force Base in Guam (a staging ground for drone flights over Asia). Other Global Hawks are stationed at Grand Forks Air Force Base in North Dakota, while the Aeronautical Systems Center at Wright-Patterson Air Force Base in Ohio manages the Global Hawk as well as the Predator and Reaper programs for the Air Force.

Other bases have been intimately involved in training drone operators, including Randolph Air Force Base in Texas and New Mexico's Kirtland Air Force Base, as is the Army's Fort Huachuca in Arizona, which is home to "the world's largest UAV training center," according to a report by *National Defense* magazine. There, hundreds of employees of defense giant General Dynamics train military personnel to fly smaller tactical drones like the Hunter and the Shadow. The physical testing of drones goes on at adjoining Libby Army Airfield and "two UAV runways located approximately four miles west of Libby," according to Global Security, an on-line clearinghouse for military information.

Additionally, small drone training for the Army is carried out at Fort Benning in Georgia while at Fort Rucker, Alabama -- "the home of Army aviation" -- the Unmanned Aircraft Systems program coordinates doctrine, strategy, and concepts pertaining to UAVs. Fort Benning has also seen the testing of true robotic drones -- which fly without human guidance or a hand on any joystick. This, wrote the *Washington Post*, is considered the next step toward a future in which drones will "hunt, identify, and kill the enemy based on calculations made by software, not decisions made by humans."

The Army has also carried out UAV training exercises at Dugway Proving Ground in Utah and, in 2011, the Navy launched its X-47B, a next-generation semi-autonomous stealth drone, on its first flight at Edwards Air Force Base in California. That flying robot --

designed to operate from the decks of aircraft carriers – was then sent on to Maryland's Naval Air Station Patuxent River for further testing. At nearby Webster Field, the Navy worked out kinks in its Fire Scout pilotless helicopter, which has also been tested at Fort Rucker and Yuma Proving Ground in Arizona, as well as Florida's Mayport Naval Station and Jacksonville Naval Air Station. The latter base was also where the Navy's Broad Area Maritime Surveillance (BAMS) unmanned aerial system was developed. It is now based there and at Naval Air Station Whidbey Island in Washington State.

Foreign Jewels in the Crown

The Navy is actively looking for a suitable site in the Western Pacific for a BAMS base, and is currently in talks with several Persian Gulf states about a site in the Middle East. It already has Global Hawks perched at its base in Sigonella, Italy.

The Air Force has relocated some of the Predator drones it previously operated in Iraq to the giant air base at Incirlik, Turkey. Many different UAVs had been based in Iraq since the American invasion of that country, including small tactical models like the Raven-B that troops launched by hand from Kirkuk Regional Air Base, Shadow UAVs that flew from Forward Operating Base Normandy in Baqubah Province, Predators operating out of Balad Airbase, miniature Desert Hawk drones launched from Tallil Air Base, and Scan Eagles based at Al Asad Air Base.

Elsewhere in the Greater Middle East, according to *Aviation Week*, the military is launching Global Hawks from Al Dhafra Air Base in the United Arab Emirates, piloted by personnel stationed at Naval Air Station Patuxent River in Maryland, to track "shipping traffic in the Persian Gulf, Strait of Hormuz, and Arabian Sea." There are unconfirmed reports that the CIA may be operating drones from the Emirates as well. In the past, other UAVs have apparently been flown from Kuwait's Ali Al Salem Air Base and Al Jaber Air Base, as well as Seeb Air Base in Oman.

At Al-Udeid Air Base in Qatar, the Air Force runs an air operations command and control facility, critical to the drone wars in Afghanistan and Pakistan. The new secret CIA base on the Arabian peninsula, used to assassinate Anwar al-Awlaki, may or may not be the airstrip in Saudi Arabia whose existence a senior U.S. military official confirmed to Fox News in October 2011. In the past, the CIA has also operated UAVs out of Tuzel, Uzbekistan.

In neighboring Afghanistan, drones fly from many bases including Jalalabad Air Base, Kandahar Air Field, the air base at Bagram, Camp Leatherneck, Camp Dwyer, Combat Outpost Payne, Forward Operating Base (FOB) Edinburgh, and FOB Delaram II, to name a few. Afghan bases are, however, more than just locations where drones take off and land.

It is a common misconception that U.S.-based operators are the only ones who "fly" America's armed drones. In fact, in and around America's war zones, UAVs begin and end their flights under the control of local "pilots." Take Afghanistan's massive Bagram Air Base. After performing preflight checks alongside a technician who focuses on the drone's sensors, a local airman sits in front of a Dell computer tower and multiple monitors, two keyboards, a joystick, a throttle, a rollerball, a mouse, and various switches, overseeing the plane's takeoff before handing it over to a stateside counterpart with a similar electronics set-up. After the mission is complete, the controls are transferred back to the local operators for the landing. Additionally, crews in Afghanistan perform general maintenance and repairs on the drones.

In the wake of a devastating suicide attack by an al-Qaeda double agent that killed CIA officers and contractors at Forward Operating Base Chapman in Afghanistan's eastern province of Khost in 2009, it came to light that the facility was heavily involved in target selection for drone strikes across the border in Pakistan. The drones themselves, as the *Washington Post* noted at the time, were "flown from separate bases in Afghanistan and Pakistan."

Both the Air Force and the CIA have conducted operations in Pakistani air space, with some missions originating in Afghanistan and others from inside Pakistan. In 2006, images of what appear to be Predator drones stationed at Shamsi Air Base in Pakistan's Balochistan province were found on Google Earth and later published. In 2009, the *New York Times* reported that operatives from Xe Services, the company formerly known as Blackwater, had taken over the task of arming Predator drones at the CIA's "hidden bases in Pakistan and Afghanistan."

Following the May Navy SEAL raid into Pakistan that killed Osama bin Laden, that country's leaders ordered the United States to leave Shamsi. The Americans reportedly did so, even though, according to the *Washington Post*, the base was actually owned and sublet to the U.S. by the United Arab Emirates, which had built the airfield "as an arrival point for falconry and other hunting expeditions in Pakistan."

The U.S. and Pakistani governments have since claimed that Shamsi is no longer being used for drone strikes. The U.S. has reportedly used other Pakistani bases for its drones, including possibly Quetta International Airport, PAF Base Chaklala, PAF Base Shahbaz, and Tarbela Ghazi Air Force Base

The New Scramble for Africa

Recently, the headline story, when it comes to the expansion of the empire of drone bases, has been Africa. For the last decade, the U.S. military has been operating out of Camp Lemonier, a former French Foreign Legion base in the tiny African nation of Djibouti. Not long after the attacks of September 11, 2001, it became a base for Predator drones and has since been used to conduct missions over neighboring Somalia.

For some time, rumors have also been circulating about a secret American base in Ethiopia. Last year, a U.S. official revealed to the *Washington Post* that discussions about a drone base there had been underway for up to four years, "but that plan was delayed because 'the Ethiopians were not all that jazzed.'" In late 2011, however, construction was evidently already underway, if not complete.

Then, of course, there is that base on the Seychelles in the Indian Ocean. A small fleet of Navy and Air Force drones began operating openly there in 2009 to track pirates in the region's waters. Classified diplomatic cables obtained by WikiLeaks, however, reveal that those drones have also secretly been used to carry out missions in Somalia. "Based in a hangar located about a quarter-mile from the main passenger terminal at the airport," the *Post* reports, the base consists of three or four "Reapers and about 100 U.S. military personnel and contractors, according to the cables."

The U.S. has also sent four smaller tactical drones to the African nations of Uganda and Burundi for use by those countries' militaries.

New and Old Empires

Even if the Pentagon budget were to begin to shrink, expansion of America's empire of drone bases is a sure thing in the years to come. Drones are now the bedrock of Washington's future military planning and -- with counterinsurgency out of favor -- the preferred way of carrying out wars abroad.

During the eight years of George W. Bush's presidency, as the U.S. was building up its drone fleets, the country launched wars in Afghanistan and Iraq, and carried out limited strikes in Yemen, Pakistan, and Somalia, using drones in at least four of those countries. In little more than three years under President Obama, the U.S. launched drone strikes in Afghanistan, Iraq, Libya, Pakistan, Somalia, Yemen, and the Philippines. It maintains that it has carte blanche to kill suspected enemies in any nation (or at least any nation in the global south).

According to a report by the Congressional Budget Office published in 2011, "the Department of Defense plans to purchase about 730 new medium-sized and large unmanned aircraft systems" over the next decade. In practical terms, this means more drones like the Reaper.

Military officials told the *Wall Street Journal* that the Reaper "can fly 1,150 miles from base, conduct missions, and return home… [T]he time a drone can stay aloft depends on how heavily armed it is." According to a drone operator training document obtained by TomDispatch, at maximum payload, meaning with 3,750 pounds worth of Hellfire missiles and GBU-12 or GBU-30 bombs on board, the Reaper can remain aloft for 16 to 20 hours.

Even a glance at a world map tells you that, if the U.S. is to carry out ever more drone strikes across the developing world, it will need more bases for its future UAVs. As an unnamed senior military official pointed out to a *Washington Post* reporter, speaking of all those new drone bases clustered around the Somali and Yemeni war zones, "If you look at it geographically, it makes sense -- you get out a ruler and draw the distances [drones] can fly and where they take off from."

An analysis by TomDispatch determined that, in 2011, there were more than 1,000 U.S. military bases scattered across the globe -- a shadowy base-world providing plenty of existing sites that can, and no doubt will, host drones. But facilities selected for a pre-drone world may not always prove optimal locations for America's current and future undeclared wars and assassination campaigns. So further expansion in Africa, the Middle East, and Asia is a likelihood.

What are the Air Force's plans in this regard? Lieutenant Colonel John Haynes was typically circumspect, saying, "We are constantly evaluating potential operating locations based on evolving mission needs." If the last decade is any indication, those "needs" will only continue to grow.

Airman 1st Class Caleb Force assists 1st Lt. Jorden Smith, a MQ-1B Predator pilot, in locating simulated targets during a training mission conducted inside the simulators at Creech Air Force Base, Nev. (U.S. Air Force photo/Senior Airman Nadine Y. Barclay)

Chapter 7

Sex and the Single Drone

Tom Engelhardt

In the world of weaponry, they are the sexiest things around. Others countries are desperate to have them. Almost anyone who writes about them becomes a groupie. Reporters exploring their onrushing future swoon at their potentially wondrous techno-talents. They are, of course, the unmanned drones, our grimly named Predators and Reapers.

The U.S. Air Force is already training more personnel to become drone "pilots" than to pilot actual planes. You don't need it in skywriting to know that, as icons of American-style war, they are clearly in our future -- and they're even heading for the homeland as police departments clamor for them.

They are relatively cheap. When they "hunt," no one dies (at least on our side). They are capable of roaming the world. Someday, they will land on the decks of aircraft carriers or, tiny as hummingbirds, drop onto a windowsill, maybe even yours, or in their hundreds, the size of bees, swarm to targets and, if all goes well, coordinate their actions using the artificial intelligence version of "hive minds."

"The drone," writes Jim Lobe of Inter Press Service, "has increasingly become the

[Obama] administration's 'weapon of choice' in its efforts to subdue al-Qaeda and its affiliates." In hundreds of attacks over the last years in the Pakistani tribal borderlands, they have killed thousands, including al-Qaeda figures, Taliban militants, and civilians. They have played a significant and growing role in the skies over Afghanistan. They are now loosing their missiles ever more often over Yemen, less often over Somalia. Their bases are spreading. No one in Congress will be able to resist them. They are defining the new world of war for the twenty-first century -- and many of the humans who theoretically command and control them can hardly keep up.

Reach for Your Dictionaries

On September 15, 2011, the *New York Times* front-paged a piece by the estimable Charlie Savage, based on leaks from inside the administration. It was headlined "At White House, Weighing Limits of Terror Fight," and started this way:

"The Obama administration's legal team is split over how much latitude the United States has to kill Islamist militants in Yemen and Somalia, a question that could define the limits of the war against al-Qaeda and its allies, according to administration and Congressional officials."

Lawyers for the Pentagon and the State Department, Savage reported, were debating whether, outside of "hot" war zones, the Obama administration could call in the drones (as well as special operations forces) not just to go after top al-Qaeda figures planning attacks on the United States, but al-Qaeda's foot soldiers (and vaguely allied groups like the Taliban in Afghanistan and Pakistan, and al-Shabab in Somalia).

That those lawyers are arguing fiercely over such a matter is certainly a curiosity. As presented, the issue behind their disagreement is how to square modern realities with outmoded rules of war written for another age (which also, by the way, had its terrorists). And yet such debates, front-paged or not, fierce or not, will one day undoubtedly be seen as analogous to supposed ancient clerical arguments over just how many angels could dance on the head of a pin. In fact, their import lies mainly in the fascinating pattern they reveal about the way forces that could care less about questions of legality are driving developments in American-style war.

After all, this fierce "argument" about what constraints should be applied to modern robotic war was first played out in the air over Pakistan's tribal borderlands. There, the CIA's drone air campaign began with small numbers of missions targeting a few highly placed al-Qaeda leaders (not terribly successfully). Rather than declare its latest wonder weapons a failure, however, the CIA, already deeply invested in drone operations, simply pushed ever harder to expand the targeting to play to the technological strengths of the planes.

In 2007, CIA director Michael Hayden began lobbying the White House for "permission to carry out strikes against houses or cars merely on the basis of behavior that matched a 'pattern of life' associated with al-Qaeda or other groups." And next thing you knew, they were moving from a few attempted targeted assassinations toward a larger air war of annihilation against types and "behaviors."

Here's another curiosity. The day after Charlie Savage's piece appeared in the *Times*, the president's top advisor on counterterror operations, John O. Brennan, gave a speech at a conference at Harvard Law School on "Strengthening our Security by Adhering to our Values and Laws," and seemed to settle the "debate," part of which he defined this way:

"Others in the international community -- including some of our closest allies and partners -- take a different view of the geographic scope of the conflict, limiting it only to the 'hot' battlefields. As such, they argue that, outside of these two active theatres, the United States can only act in self-defense against al-Qaeda when they are planning, engaging in, or threatening an armed attack against U.S. interests if it amounts to an 'imminent' threat."

He then added this little twist: "Practically speaking, then, the question turns principally on how you define 'imminence.'"

If there's one thing we should have learned from the Bush years, it was this: when government officials reach for their dictionaries, duck!

Then, the crucial word at stake was "torture," and faced with it -- and what top administration officials actually wanted done in the world -- Justice Department lawyers quite literally reached for their dictionaries. In their infamous torture memos, they so pretzled, abused, and redefined the word "torture" that, by the time they were through, whether acts of torture even occurred was left to the torturer, to what had he had in mind when he was "interrogating" someone. ("[I]f a defendant [interrogator] has a good faith belief that his actions will not result in prolonged mental harm, he lacks the mental state necessary for his actions to constitute torture.")

As a result, "torture" was essentially drummed out of the dictionary (except when committed by heinous evil doers in places like Iran) and "enhanced interrogation techniques" welcomed into our world. The Bush administration and the CIA then proceeded to fill the "black sites" they set up from Poland to Thailand and the torture chambers of chummy regimes like Mubarak's Egypt and Gaddafi's Libya with "terror suspects," and then tortured away with impunity.

Now, it seems, the Obama crowd is reaching for its dictionaries, which means that it's undoubtedly time to duck again. As befits a more intellectual crowd, we're no longer talking about relatively simple words like "torture" whose meaning everyone knows (or at least once knew). If "imminence" is now the standard for when robotic war is really war, don't you yearn for the good old days when the White House focused on "what the meaning of the word 'is' is," and all that was at stake was presidential sex, not presidential killing?

When legalisms take center stage in a situation like this, think of magicians. Their skill is to focus your attention on the space where nothing that matters is happening -- the wrong hand, the wrong face, the wrong part of the stage -- while they perform their "magic" elsewhere. Similarly, pay attention to the law right now and you're likely to miss the plot line of our world.

It's true that, at the moment, articles are pouring out focused on how to define the limits of future drone warfare. My advice: skip the law, skip the definitions, skip the arguments, and focus your attention on the drones and the people developing them instead.

Put another way, in the last decade, there was only one definition that truly mattered. From it everything else followed: the almost instantaneous post-9/11 insistence that we were "at war," and not even in a specific war or set of wars, but in an all-encompassing one that, within two weeks of the collapse of the World Trade Center, President Bush was already calling "the war on terror." That single demonic definition of our state of existence rose to mind so quickly that no lawyers were needed and no one had to reach for a dictionary.

Addressing a joint session of Congress, the president typically said: "Our war on terror begins with Al Qaeda, but it does not end there." And that open-endedness was soon codified in an official name that told all: "the Global War on Terror," or GWOT. (For all we know, the phrase itself was the invention of a speechwriter mainlining into the *zeitgeist*.) Suddenly, "sovereignty" had next to no meaning (if you weren't a superpower); the U.S. was ready to take out after terrorists in up to 80 countries; and the planet, by definition, had become a global free-fire zone.

By the end of September 2001, as the invasion of Afghanistan was being prepared, it was already a carte-blanche world and, as it happened, pilotless surveillance drones were there, lurking in the shadows, waiting for a moment like this, yearning (you might say) to be weaponized.

If GWOT preceded much thought of drones, it paved the way for their crash weaponization, development, and deployment. It was no mistake that, a bare two weeks after 9/11, a prescient Noah Shachtman (who would go on to found the Danger Room website at *Wired*) led off a piece for that magazine this way: "Unmanned, almost disposable spy planes are being groomed for a major role in the coming conflict against terrorism, defense analysts say."

Talk about "imminence" or "constraints" all you want, but as long as we are "at war," not just in Afghanistan or Iraq, but on a world scale with something known as "terror," there will never be any limits, other than self-imposed ones.

And it remains so today, even though the Obama administration has long avoided the term "Global War on Terror." As Brennan made utterly clear in his speech, President Obama considers us "at war" anywhere that al-Qaeda, its minions, wannabes, or simply groups of irregulars we don't much care for may be located. Given this mentality, there is little reason to believe that, on September 11, 2021, we won't still be "at war."

So pay no attention to the legalisms. Put away those dictionaries. Ignore the "debates" between the White House and Congress, or State and Defense. Otherwise you'll miss the predatory magic.

Beyond Words

Within days after the news about the "debate" over the limits on global war was leaked to the *Times*, unnamed government officials were leaking away to the *Washington Post* and the *Wall Street Journal* on an allied subject of interest. Both papers broke the news that, as Craig Whitlock and Greg Miller of the *Post* put it, the U.S. military and the CIA were creating "a constellation of secret drone bases for counterterrorism operations in the Horn of Africa and the Arabian Peninsula as part of a newly aggressive campaign to attack al-Qaeda affiliates in Somalia and Yemen."

These preparations are meant to deal not just with Washington's present preoccupations, but with its future fears and phantasms. In this way, they fit well with the now decade-old war on terror's campaign against will-o-the-wisps. Julian Barnes of the *Wall Street Journal*, for example, quotes an unnamed "senior U.S. official" as saying: "We do not know enough about the leaders of the al-Qaeda affiliates in Africa. Is there a guy out there saying, 'I am the future of al-Qaeda'? Who is the next Osama bin Laden?" We don't yet know, but wherever he is, our drones will be ready for him.

All of this, in turn, fits well with the Pentagon's "legal" position, mentioned by the *Times'* Savage, of "trying to maintain maximum theoretical flexibility." It's a kind of Field-of-Dreams argument: if you build them, they will come.

It's simple enough. The machines (and their creators and supporters in the military-industrial complex) are decades ahead of the government officials who theoretically direct and oversee them. "A Future for Drones: Automated Killing," an enthusiastic article that appeared in the *Post* the very same week as that paper's base-expansion piece, caught the spirit of the moment. In it, Peter Finn reported on the way three pilotless drones over Fort Benning, Georgia, worked together to identify a target without human guidance. It may, he wrote, "presage the future of the American way of war: a day when drones hunt, identify, and kill the enemy based on calculations made by software, not decisions made by humans. Imagine aerial 'Terminators,' minus beefcake and time travel."

In a *New York Review of Books* piece with a similarly admiring edge (and who wouldn't admire such staggering technological advances), Christian Caryl writes:

"Researchers are now testing UAVs [unmanned aerial vehicles] that mimic hummingbirds or seagulls; one model under development can fit on a pencil eraser. There is much speculation about linking small drones or robots together into 'swarms' -- clouds or crowds of machines that would share their intelligence, like a hive mind, and have the capability to converge instantly on identified targets. This might seem like science fiction, but it is probably not that far away."

Admittedly, drones still can't have sex. Not yet anyway. And they can't choose which humans they are sent to kill. Not so far. But sex and the single drone aside, all of this and more may, in the coming decades, become -- if you don't mind my using the word -- imminent. It may be the reality in the skies over all our heads.

It's true that the machines of war the Obama administration is now rushing headlong to deploy cannot yet operate themselves, but they are already -- in Ralph Waldo Emerson's words -- "in the saddle, and ride mankind." Their "desire" to be deployed and used is driving policy in Washington -- and increasingly elsewhere as well. Think of this as the Drone Imperative.

If you want to fight over definitions, there's only one worth fighting over: not the phrase "the Global War on Terror," which the Obama administration tossed aside to no effect whatsoever, but the concept behind it. Once the idea took hold that the United States was, and had no choice but to be, in a state of permanent global war, the game was afoot. From then on, the planet was -- conceptually speaking -- a free-fire zone, and even before robotic weaponry developed to its present level, it was already a drone-eat-drone world to the horizon.

As long as global war remains the essence of "foreign policy," the drones -- and the military-industrial companies and lobbying groups behind them, as well as the military and CIA careers being built on them -- will prove expansive. They will go where, and as far as, the technology takes them.

In reality, it's not the drones, but our leaders who are remarkably constrained. Out of permanent war and terrorism, they have built a house with no doors and no exits. It's easy enough to imagine them as beleaguered masters of the universe atop the globe's military superpower, but in terms of what they can actually do, it would be more practical to think of them as so many drones, piloted by others. In truth, our present leaders, or rather managers, are small people operating on autopilot in a big-machine world.

As they definitionally twitch and turn, we can just begin to glimpse -- like an old-fashioned photo developing in a tray of chemicals -- the outlines of a new form of American imperial war emerging before our eyes. It involves guarding the empire on the cheap, as well as on the sly, via the CIA, which has, in recent years, developed into a full-scale, drone-heavy paramilitary outfit, via a growing secret army of special operations forces that has been incubating inside the military these last years, and of course via those missile- and bomb-armed robotic assassins of the sky.

The appeal is obvious: the cost (in U.S. lives) is low; in the case of the drones, nonexistent. There is no need for large counterinsurgency armies of occupation of the sort that have bogged down on the mainland of the Greater Middle East these last years.

In an increasingly cash-strapped and anxious Washington, it must look like a literal godsend. How could it go wrong?

Of course, that's a thought you can only hang onto as long as you're looking down on a planet filled with potential targets scurrying below you. The minute you look up, the minute you leave your joystick and screen behind and begin to imagine yourself on the ground, it's obvious how things could go so very, very wrong -- how, in fact, in Pakistan, to take but one example, they are going so very, very wrong.

Just think about the last time you went to a *Terminator* film: Who did you identify with? John and Sarah Connor, or the implacable terminators chasing them? And you don't need artificial intelligence to grasp why in a nanosecond.

In a country now struggling simply to guarantee help to its own citizens struck by natural disasters, Washington is preparing distinctly unnatural disasters in the imperium. In this way, both at home and abroad, the American dream is turning into the American scream.

So when we build those bases on that global field of screams, when we send our armadas of drones out to kill, don't be surprised if the rest of the world doesn't see us as the good guys or the heroes, but as terminators. It's not the best way to make friends and influence people, but once your mindset is permanent war, that's no longer a priority. It's a scream, and there's nothing funny about it.

Aircraft mechanics replace a multi-spectural targeting system ball on an MQ-1B Predator at Ali Base, Iraq. (U.S. Air Force photo/Tech. Sgt. Sabrina Johnson)

Chapter 8

The Life and Death of American Drones

Nick Turse

The drone had been in the air for close to five hours before its mission crew realized that something was wrong. The oil temperature in the plane's turbocharger, they noticed, had risen into the "cautionary" range. An hour later, it was worse, and it just kept rising as the minutes wore on. While the crew desperately ran through its "engine overheat" checklist trying to figure out the problem, the engine oil temperature, too, began skyrocketing.

By now, they had a full-blown in-flight emergency on their hands. "We still have control of the engine, but engine failure is imminent," the pilot announced over the radio.

Almost two hours after the first signs of distress, the engine indeed failed. Traveling at 712 feet per minute, the drone clipped a fence before crashing.

Land of the Lost Drones

The skies seem full of falling drones these days. The most publicized of them made headlines when Iran announced that its military had taken possession of an advanced

American remotely piloted spy aircraft, thought to be an RQ-170 Sentinel.

Questions about how the Iranians came to possess one of the U.S. military's most sophisticated pieces of equipment abound. Iran first claimed that its forces shot the drone down after it "briefly violated" the country's eastern airspace near the Afghan border. Later, the Islamic Republic insisted that the unmanned aerial vehicle had penetrated 150 miles before being felled by a sophisticated cyber-attack. And then, an Iranian engineer offered a more detailed, but unsubstantiated explanation of how a hack-attack hijacked the aircraft.

For its part, the United States initially claimed that its military had lost the drone while it was on a mission in western Afghanistan. Later, unnamed officials admitted that the CIA had, in fact, been conducting a covert spy operation over Iran.

The drone crash that began this chapter did occur in Afghanistan -- Kandahar, to be precise -- in May of 2011. It went unreported at the time and involved not a sleek, bat-winged RQ-170 Sentinel, but the older, clunkier, if more famous, MQ-1 Predator, a workhorse hunter/killer machine of the Afghan war and the CIA's drone assassination campaign in the Pakistani tribal borderlands.

A document detailing a U.S. Air Force investigation of that Predator crash, examined by TomDispatch, sheds light on the lifecycle and flaws of drones -- just what can go wrong in unmanned air operations -- as well as the shadowy system of bases and units scattered across the globe that keep those drones constantly in the skies as the U.S. becomes ever more reliant on remote-controlled warfare.

That report and striking new statistics obtained from the military offer insights into underexamined flaws in drone technology. They should be, among other things, a reminder of the failure of journalists to move beyond awe when it comes to high-tech warfare and America's latest wonder weapons -- their curious inability to examine the stark limitations of man and machine that can send even the most advanced military technology hurtling to Earth.

Numbers Game

According to statistics provided to TomDispatch by the Air Force, Predators have flown the lion's share of hours in America's drone wars. As of October 1, 2011, MQ-1's had spent more than 1 million hours in the air, 965,000 of those in "combat," since being introduced into military service. The newer, more heavily armed MQ-9 Reaper, by comparison, has flown 215,000 hours, 180,000 of them in combat. (The Air Force refuses to release information about the workload of the RQ-170 Sentinel.) And these numbers continue to rise. In 2011 alone, Predators logged 228,000 flight hours compared to 190,000 the previous year.

An analysis of official Air Force data conducted by TomDispatch indicates that its drones crashed in spectacular fashion no less than 13 times in 2011, including that May 5th crash in Kandahar.

About half of those mishaps, all resulting in the loss of an aircraft or property damage of $2 million or more, occurred in Afghanistan or in the tiny African nation of Djibouti, which serves as a base for drones involved in the U.S. secret wars in Somalia and Yemen. All but two of the incidents involved the MQ-1 model, and four of them took place in May.

In 2010, there were at least seven major drone mishaps, all but one involving Predators; in 2009, there were 11. In other words, there have been no less than 31 drone losses in three years, none apparently shot down by enemy fire.

Other publicized drone crashes, like a remotely-operated Navy helicopter that went down in Libya in June and an unmanned aerial vehicle whose camera was reportedly taken by Afghan insurgents after a crash in August, as well as the December 2011 loss of the RQ-180 in Iran and the crash of an MQ-9 in the Seychelles, are not included in the Air Force's major accident statistics.

Group Effort

The May 5, 2011 Predator crash about a half-mile short of a runway at Kandahar Air Field drives home just how diffuse drone operations have become, with multiple units and multiple bases playing a role in a single mission.

That Predator drone, for example, was an asset of the 3rd Special Operations Squadron, which operates out of Cannon Air Force Base in New Mexico, and ultimately is part of Air Force Special Operations Command, based at Hurlburt Field in Florida. When it crashed, it was being flown by an in-country pilot from the 62nd Expeditionary Squadron at Kandahar Air Field, whose parent unit, the 18th Reconnaissance Squadron, makes its home at Creech Air Force Base in Nevada, ground zero for the military's drone operations. The crewman operating the sensors on the drone, on the other hand, was a member of the Texas Air National Guard based at Ellington Field in Texas.

The final leg of the doomed mission -- in support of elite special operations forces -- was being carried out by a pilot who had been operating Predators for about 10 months and had flown drones for approximately 51 hours over the previous 90 days. With less than 400 total hours under his belt, he was considered "inexperienced" by Air Force standards and, during his drone launch and recovery training, had failed two simulator sessions and one flying exercise. He had, however, excelled academically, passed his evaluations, and was considered a qualified MQ-1 pilot, cleared to fly without supervision.

His sensor operator had been qualified by the Air Force for the better part of two years, with average or above average ratings in performance evaluations. Having "flown" a total of 677 hours -- close to 50 of them in the 90 days before the crash -- he was considered "experienced."

The fact that the duo were controlling a special operations drone highlights the increasingly strong and symbiotic relationship between America's two recently ascendant forms of warfare: raids by small teams of elite forces and attacks by remote-controlled robots.

The Life and Death of American Drones

During the post-crash investigation, it was determined that the ground crew in Afghanistan had been regularly using an unauthorized method of draining engine coolant, though it was unclear whether this contributed to the crash. Investigation documents further indicated that the drone's engine had 851 hours of flight time and so was nearing the end of the line. (The operational lifespan of a Predator drone engine is reportedly around 1,080 hours.)

Following the crash, the engine was shipped to a California test facility, where technicians from General Atomics, the maker of the Predator, carried out a forensic investigation. Significant overheating had, it was discovered, warped and deformed the machinery.

Eventually, the Air Force ruled that a cooling system malfunction had led to engine failure. An accident investigator also concluded that the pilot had not executed proper procedures after the engine failure, causing the craft to crash just short of the runway, slightly damaging the perimeter fence at Kandahar Air Field and destroying the drone.

The clear conclusion reached by accident investigators in this crash stands in stark contrast to the murkiness of what happened to the advanced drone that ended up in Iranian hands. Whether the latter crashed thanks to a malfunction, was shot down, felled by a cyber-attack, or ended up on the ground for some other reason entirely, its loss and that of the special ops drone are reminders of just how reliant the U.S. military has become on high-tech robot planes whose major accidents now exceed those of much more expensive fixed-wing aircraft. (There were 10 major airborne mishaps involving such Air Force aircraft in 2011.)

Robot War: 2012 and Beyond

The failure to achieve victory in Iraq and Afghanistan, combined with a perceived success in the Libyan war -- significantly fought with airpower including drones -- has convinced many in the military not to abandon foreign wars, but to change their approach.

Long-term occupations involving tens of thousands of troops and the use of counterinsurgency tactics are to be traded in for drone and special forces operations.

Remotely piloted aircraft have regularly been touted, in the press and the military, as wonder weapons, the way, not so long ago, counterinsurgency tactics were being promoted as an elixir for military failure. Like the airplane, the tank, and nuclear weapons before it, the drone has been hailed as a game-changer, destined to alter the very essence of warfare.

Instead, like the others, it has increasingly proven to be a non-game-changer of a weapon with ordinary vulnerabilities. Its technology is fallible and its efforts have often been counterproductive in these last years. For example, the inability of pilots watching computer monitors on the other side of the planet to discriminate between armed combatants and innocent civilians has proven a continuing problem for the military's drone operations, while the CIA's judge-jury-executioner assassination program is widely considered to have run afoul of international law -- and, in the case of Pakistan, to be alienating an entire population. The drone increasingly looks less like a winning weapon than a machine for generating opposition and enemies.

In addition, as flight hours rise year after year, the vulnerabilities of remotely piloted missions are ever more regularly coming to light. These have included Iraqi insurgents hacking drone video feeds, a virulent computer virus infecting the Air Force's unmanned fleet, large percentages of drone pilots suffering from "high operational stress," increasing numbers of crashes, and the possibility of Iranian drone-hijacking.

While human and mechanical errors are inherent in the operation of any type of machinery, few commentators have focused significant attention on the full spectrum of drone flaws and limitations. For more than a decade, remotely piloted aircraft have been a mainstay of U.S. military operations and the tempo of drone operations continues to rise yearly, but relatively little has been written about drone defects or the limits and hazards of drone operations.

Perhaps the Air Force is beginning to worry about when this will change. After years of regularly ushering reporters through drone operations at Creech Air Force Base and getting a flood of glowing, even awestruck, publicity about the glories of drones and drone pilots, in 2011, without explanation, it shut down press access to the program, moving robotic warfare deeper into the shadows.

The losses of the Pentagon's robot Sentinel in Iran, the Reaper in the Seychelles, and the Predator in Kandahar, however, offer a window into a future in which the global skies will be filled with drones that may prove far less wondrous than Americans have been led to believe. The United States could turn out to be relying on a fleet of robots with wings of clay.

RQ-4 Global Hawk maintenance Airmen with the 380th Expeditionary Aircraft Maintenance Squadron (U.S. Air Force photo/Master Sgt. Scott T. Sturkol)

Chapter 9

Offshore Everywhere

Tom Engelhardt

Make no mistake: we're entering a new world of military planning. Admittedly, the latest proposed Pentagon budget manages to preserve just about every costly toy-cum-boondoggle from the good old days when MiGs still roamed the skies, including an uncut nuclear arsenal. Eternally over-budget items like the F-35 Joint Strike Fighter, cherished by their services and well-lobbied congressional representatives, aren't leaving the scene any time soon, though delays or cuts in purchase orders are planned. All this should reassure us that, despite the talk of massive cuts, the U.S. military will continue to be the profligate, inefficient, and remarkably ineffective institution we've come to know and squander our treasure on.

Still, the cuts that matter are already in the works, the ones that will change the American way of war. They may mean little in monetary terms -- the Pentagon budget is actually slated to increase through 2017 -- but in imperial terms they will make a difference. A new way of preserving the embattled idea of an American planet is coming into focus and one thing is clear: in the name of Washington's needs, it will offer a direct challenge to national sovereignty.

Heading Offshore

When the Marines began huge amphibious exercises -- dubbed Bold Alligator 2012 -- off the east coast of the U.S. in February, someone should have IM'ed them: it won't help. No matter what they do, they are going to have fewer boots on the ground in the future, and there's going to be less ground to have them on. The same is true for the Army (even if a cut of 100,000 troops will still leave the combined forces of the two services larger than they were on September 11, 2001). Less troops, less full-frontal missions, no full-scale invasions, no more counterinsurgency: that's the order of the day. In that same month, in fact, Secretary of Defense Leon Panetta suggested that the schedule for the drawdown of combat boots in Afghanistan might be speeded up by more than a year. Consider it a sign of the times.

Like the F-35, American mega-bases, essentially well-fortified American towns plunked down in a strange land, like our latest "embassies" the size of lordly citadels, aren't going away soon. After all, in base terms, we're already hunkered down in the Greater Middle East in an impressive way. Even in post-withdrawal Iraq, the Pentagon is reportedly still trying to negotiate for a new long-term defense agreement that might include getting a little of its former base space back, and it continues to build in Afghanistan. Meanwhile, Washington has typically signaled in recent years that it's ready to fight to the last

Japanese prime minister not to lose a single base among the three dozen it has on the Japanese island of Okinawa.

But here's the thing: even if the U.S. military is dragging its old habits, weaponry, and global-basing ideas behind it, it's still heading offshore. There will be no more land wars on the Eurasian continent. Instead, greater emphasis will be placed on the Navy, the Air Force, and a policy "pivot" to face China in southern Asia where the American military position can be strengthened without more giant bases or monster embassies.

For Washington, "offshore" means the world's boundary-less waters and skies, but also, more metaphorically, it means being repositioned off the coast of national sovereignty and all its knotty problems. This change, on its way for years, will officially rebrand the planet as an American free-fire zone, unchaining Washington from the limits that national borders once imposed. New ways to cross borders and new technology for doing it without permission are clearly in the planning stages, and U.S. forces are being reconfigured accordingly.

Think of the raid that killed Osama bin Laden as a harbinger of and model for what's to come. It was an operation enveloped in a cloak of secrecy. There was no consultation with the "ally" on whose territory the raid was to occur. It involved combat by an elite special operations unit backed by drones and other high-tech weaponry and supported by the CIA. A national boundary was crossed without either permission or any declaration of hostilities. The object was that elusive creature "terrorism," the perfect global will-o'-the-wisp around which to plan an offshore future.

All the elements of this emerging formula for retaining planetary dominance have received plenty of publicity, but the degree to which they combine to assault traditional concepts of national sovereignty has been given little attention.

Since November 2002, when a Hellfire missile from a CIA-operated Predator drone turned a car with six alleged al-Qaeda operatives in Yemen into ash, robotic aircraft have led the way in this border-crossing, air-space penetrating assault. The U.S. now has drone bases across the planet. Increasingly, the long-range reach of its drone program means that those robotic planes can penetrate just about any nation's air space. It matters little whether that country houses them itself. Take Pakistan, which forced the CIA to remove its drones from Shamsi Air Base as 2011 ended. Nonetheless, CIA drone strikes in that country's tribal borderlands continue, assumedly from bases in Afghanistan, and recently President Obama offered a full-throated public defense of them. (That there have been fewer of them lately has been a political decision of the Obama administration, not of the Pakistanis.)

Drones themselves are distinctly fallible, crash-prone machines. (In a single week early in 2012, for instance, an advanced Israeli drone capable of hitting Iran went down on a test flight, a surveillance drone -- assumedly American -- crashed in a Somali refugee camp, and a report surfaced that some U.S. drones in Afghanistan can't fly in that country's summer heat.) Still, they are, relatively speaking, cheap to produce. They can fly long distances across almost any border with no danger whatsoever to their human pilots and are capable of staying aloft for extended periods of time. They allow for surveillance and strikes anywhere. By their nature, they are border-busting creatures. It's no mistake then that they are winners in the latest Pentagon budgeting battles or, as a headline at *Wired's* Danger Room blog summed matters up, "Humans Lose, Robots Win in New Defense Budget."

And keep in mind that when drones are capable of taking off from and landing on aircraft carrier decks, they will quite literally be offshore with respect to all borders, but capable of crossing any. (The Navy's latest plans include a future drone that will land itself on those decks without a human pilot at any controls.)

War has always been the most human *and* inhuman of activities. Now, it seems, its inhuman aspect is quite literally on the rise. With the U.S. military working to roboticize the future battlefield, the American way of war is destined to be imbued with *Terminator*-style terror.

Already American drones regularly cross borders with mayhem in mind in Pakistan, Somalia, and Yemen. Because of a drone downed in Iran, we know that they have also been flying surveillance missions in that country's airspace as -- for the State Department -- they are in Iraq. Washington is undoubtedly planning for far more of the same.

American War Enters the Shadows

Along with those skies filled with increasing numbers of drones goes a rise in U.S. special operations forces. They, too, are almost by definition boundary-busting outfits. Once upon a time, an American president had his own "private army" -- the CIA. Now, in a sense, he has his own private military. Formerly modest-sized units of elite special operations forces have grown into a force of 60,000, a secret military cocooned in the military, which is slated for further expansion. According to Nick Turse, in 2011 special operations units were in 120 nations, almost two-thirds of the countries on Earth.

By their nature, special operations forces work in the shadows: as hunter-killer teams, night raiders, and border-crossers. They function in close conjunction with drones and, as the regular Army slowly withdraws from its giant garrisons in places like Europe, they are preparing to operate in a new world of stripped-

118

down bases called "lily pads" -- think frogs jumping across a pond to their prey. No longer will the Pentagon be building American towns with all the amenities of home, but forward-deployed, minimalist outposts near likely global hotspots, like Camp Lemonnier in the North African nation of Djibouti.

Increasingly, American war itself will enter those shadows, where crossings of every sort of border, domestic as well as foreign, are likely to take place with little accountability to anyone, except the president and the national security complex.

In those shadows, our secret forces are already melding into one another. A striking sign of this was the appointment as CIA director of a general who, in Iraq and Afghanistan, had relied heavily on special forces hunter-killer teams and night raiders, as well as drones, to do the job. Undoubtedly the most highly praised general of our American moment, General David Petraeus has himself slipped into the shadows where he is presiding over covert civilian forces working ever more regularly in tandem with special operations teams and sharing drone assignments with the military.

And don't forget the Navy, which couldn't be more offshore to begin with. It already operates 11 aircraft carrier task forces (none of which are to be cut -- thanks to a decision reportedly made by the president). These are, effectively, major American bases -- massively armed small American towns -- at sea. To these, the Navy is adding smaller "bases." Right now, for instance, it's retrofitting an old amphibious transport docking ship bound for the Persian Gulf either as a Navy Seal commando "mothership" or (depending on which Pentagon spokesperson you listen to) as a "lily pad" for counter-mine Sikorsky MH-53 helicopters and patrol craft. Whichever it may be, it will just be a stopgap until the Navy can build new "Afloat Forward Staging Bases" from scratch.

Futuristic weaponry now in the planning stages could add to the military's border-crossing capabilities. Take the Army's Advanced Hypersonic Weapon or DARPA's Falcon Hypersonic Technology Vehicle 2, both of which are intended, someday, to hit targets anywhere on Earth with massive conventional explosives in less than an hour.

From lily pads to aircraft carriers, advanced drones to special operations teams, it's offshore and into the shadows for U.S. military policy. While the United States is economically in decline, it remains the sole military superpower on the planet. No other country pours anywhere near as much money into its military and its national security establishment or is likely to do so in the foreseeable future. It's clear enough that Washington is hoping to offset any economic decline with newly reconfigured military might. As in the old TV show, the U.S. has gun, will travel.

Onshore, American power in the twenty-first century proved a disaster. Offshore, with Washington in control of the global seas and skies, with its ability to kick down the world's doors and strike just about anywhere without a by-your-leave or thank-you-ma'am, it hopes for better. As the early attempts to put this program into operation from Pakistan to Yemen have indicated, however, be careful what you wish for: it sometimes comes home to bite you.

Chapter 10

The Crash and Burn Future of Robot Warfare

Nick Turse

American fighter jets screamed over the Iraqi countryside heading for the MQ-1 Predator drone, while its crew in California stood by helplessly. What had begun as an ordinary reconnaissance mission was now taking a ruinous turn. In an instant, the jets attacked and then it was all over. The Predator had been obliterated.

An account of the spectacular end of that nearly $4 million drone in November 2007 is contained in a collection of Air Force accident investigation documents examined by TomDispatch. They catalog more than 70 catastrophic Air Force drone mishaps since 2000, each resulting in the loss of an aircraft or property damage of $2 million or more.

These official reports, some obtained by TomDispatch through the Freedom of Information Act, offer new insights into a largely covert, yet highly touted war-fighting, assassination, and spy program involving armed robots that are significantly less reliable than previously acknowledged. Collectively, the Air Force documents offer a remarkable portrait of modern drone warfare, one rarely found in a decade of generally triumphalist or awestruck press accounts that seldom mention the limitations of drones, much less their mission failures.

The aerial disasters described draw attention not only to the technical limitations of drone warfare, but to larger conceptual flaws inherent in such operations. Launched and landed by aircrews close to battlefields in places like Afghanistan, the drones are controlled during missions by pilots and sensor operators -- often multiple teams over many hours -- from bases in places like Nevada and North Dakota. They are sometimes also monitored by "screeners" from private security contractors at stateside bases like Hurlburt Field in Florida. (A McClatchy report revealed that it takes nearly 170 people to keep a single Predator in the air for 24 hours.)

In other words, drone missions, like the robots themselves, have many moving parts and much, it turns out, can and does go wrong. In that November 2007 Predator incident in Iraq, for instance, an electronic failure caused the robotic aircraft to engage its self-destruct mechanism and crash, after which U.S. jets destroyed the wreckage to prevent it from falling into enemy hands. In other cases, drones -- officially known as remotely piloted aircraft, or RPAs -- broke down, escaped human control and oversight, or self-destructed for reasons ranging from pilot error and bad weather to mechanical failure in Afghanistan, Djibouti, the Gulf of Aden, Iraq, Kuwait, and various other unspecified or classified foreign locations, as well as in the United States.

In 2001, Air Force Predator drones flew 7,500 hours. By the close of 2011, that number topped 70,000. As the tempo of robotic air operations has steadily increased, crashes have, not surprisingly, become more frequent. In 2001, just two Air Force drones were destroyed in accidents. In 2008, eight drones fell from the sky. Last year, the number reached 13. (Accident rates are, however, dropping according to an Air Force report relying on figures from 2009.)

Keep in mind that the 70-plus accidents recorded in those Air Force documents represent only drone crashes investigated by the Air Force under a rigid set of rules. Many other drone mishaps have not been included in the Air Force statistics.

You Don't Need a Weatherman... Or Do You?

How missions are carried out -- and sometimes fail -- is apparent from the declassified reports, including one provided to TomDispatch by the Air Force detailing a June 2011 crash. Late that month, a Predator drone took off from Jalalabad Air Base in Afghanistan to carry out a surveillance mission in support of ground forces. Piloted by a member of the 432nd Air Expeditionary Wing out of Whiteman Air Force Base in Missouri, the robotic craft ran into rough weather, causing the pilot to ask for permission to abandon the troops below.

His commander never had a chance to respond. Lacking weather avoidance equipment found on more sophisticated aircraft or on-board sensors to clue the pilot in to rapidly deteriorating meteorological conditions, and with a sandstorm interfering with ground radar, "severe weather effects" overtook the Predator. In an instant, the satellite link between pilot and plane was severed. When it momentarily flickered back to life, the crew could see that the drone was in an extreme nosedive. They then lost the datalink for a second and final time. A few minutes later, troops on the ground radioed in to say that the $4 million drone had crashed near them.

A month earlier, a Predator drone took off from the tiny African nation of Djibouti in support of Operation Enduring Freedom, which includes operations in Afghanistan as well as Yemen, Djibouti, and Somalia, among other nations. According to documents obtained via the Freedom of Information Act, about eight hours into the flight, the mission crew noticed a slow oil leak. Ten hours later, they handed the drone off to a local aircrew whose assignment was to land it at Djibouti's Ambouli Airport, a joint civilian/military facility adjacent to Camp Lemonier, a U.S. base in the country.

That mission crew -- both the pilot and sensor operator -- had been deployed from Creech Air Force Base in Nevada and had logged a combined 1,700 hours flying Predators. They were considered "experienced" by the Air Force. On this day, however, the electronic sensors that measure their drone's altitude were inaccurate, while low clouds and high humidity affected its infrared sensors and set the stage for disaster.

An investigation eventually found that, had the crew performed proper instrument cross-checks, they would have noticed a 300 to 400 foot discrepancy in their altitude. Instead, only when the RPA broke through the clouds did the sensor operator realize just how close to the ground it was. Six seconds later, the drone crashed to earth, destroying itself and one of its Hellfire missiles.

Storms, clouds, humidity, and human error aren't the only natural dangers for drones. In a November 2008 incident, a mission crew at Kandahar Air Field launched a Predator on a windy day. Just five minutes into the flight, with the aircraft still above the sprawling American mega-base, the pilot realized that the plane had already deviated from its intended course. To get it back on track, he initiated a turn that -- due to the aggressive nature of the maneuver, wind conditions, drone design, and the unbalanced weight of a missile on just one wing -- sent the plane into a roll. Despite the pilot's best efforts, the craft entered a tailspin, crashed on the base, and burst into flames.

Going Rogue

On occasion, RPAs have simply escaped from human control. Over the course of eight hours on a late February day in 2009, for example, five different crews passed off the controls of a Predator drone, one to the next, as it flew over Iraq. Suddenly, without warning, the last of them, members of the North Dakota Air National Guard at Hector International Airport in Fargo, lost communication with the plane. At that point no one -- not the pilot, nor the sensor operator, nor a local mission crew -- knew where the drone was or what it was doing. Neither transmitting nor receiving data or commands, it had, in effect, gone rogue. Only later was it determined that a datalink failure had triggered the drone's self-destruct mechanism, sending it into an unrecoverable tailspin and crash within 10 minutes of escaping human control.

In November 2009, a Predator launched from Kandahar Air Field in Afghanistan lost touch with its human handlers 20 minutes after takeoff and simply disappeared. When the mission crew was unable to raise the drone, datalink specialists were brought in but failed to find the errant plane. Meanwhile, air traffic controllers, who had lost the plane on radar, could not even locate its transponder signal. Numerous efforts to make contact failed. Two days later, at the moment the drone would have run out of fuel, the Air Force declared the Predator "lost." It took eight days for its wreckage to be located.

Crash Course

In mid-August 2004, while drone operations in the Central Command (CENTCOM) area of responsibility were running at high tempo, a Predator mission crew began hearing a cascade of warning alarms indicating engine and alternator failure, as well as a possible engine fire. When the sensor operator used his camera to scan the aircraft, it didn't take long to spot the problem. Its tail had burst into flames. Shortly afterward, it became uncontrollable and crashed.

In January 2007, a Predator drone was flying somewhere in the CENTCOM region (above one of 20 countries in the Greater Middle East). About 14 hours into a 20-hour mission, the aircraft began to falter. For 15 minutes its engine was failing, but the information it was sending back remained within normal parameters, so the mission crew failed to notice. Only at the last minute did they become aware that their drone was dying. As an investigation later determined, an expanding crack in the drone's crankshaft caused the engine to seize up. The pilot put the aircraft into a glide toward an unpopulated area. Higher headquarters then directed that he should intentionally crash it, since a rapid reaction force would not be able to reach it quickly and it was carrying two Hellfire missiles as well as unspecified "classified equipment." Days later, its remains were recovered.

The Crash and Burn Future of Robot Warfare

In spite of all the technical limitations of remote-controlled war spelled out in the Air Force investigation files, the U.S. is doubling down on drones. Under the president's new military strategy, the Air Force is projected to see its share of the budgetary pie rise and flying robots are expected to be a major part of that expansion.

Already, counting the Army's thousands of tiny drones, one in three military aircraft -- close to 7,500 machines -- are robots. According to official figures provided to TomDispatch, roughly 285 of them are Air Force Predator, Reaper, or Global Hawk drones. The Air Force's arsenal also includes more advanced Sentinels, Avengers, and other classified unmanned aircraft. A report published by the Congressional Budget Office last year, revealed that "the Department of Defense plans to purchase about 730 new medium-sized and large unmanned aircraft systems" during the next 10 years.

Over the last decade, the United States has increasingly turned to drones in an effort to win its wars. The Air Force investigation files examined by TomDispatch suggest a more extensive use of drones in Iraq than has previously been reported. But in Iraq, as in Afghanistan, America's preeminent wonder weapon failed to bring the U.S. mission anywhere close to victory. Effective as the spearhead of a program to cripple al-Qaeda in Pakistan, drone warfare in that country's tribal borderlands has also alienated almost the entire population of 190 million. In other words, an estimated 2,000 suspected or identified guerrillas (as well as untold numbers of civilians) died. The populace of a key American ally grew ever more hostile and no one knows how many new militants in search of revenge the drone strikes may have created, though the numbers are believed to be significant.

Despite a decade of technological, tactical, and strategic refinements and improvements, Air Force and allied CIA personnel watching computer monitors in distant locations have continually failed to discriminate between armed combatants and innocent civilians. In addition, drone warfare seems to be creating a sinister system of embedded economic incentives that may lead to increasing casualty figures on the ground.

"In some targeting programs, staffers have review quotas -- that is, they must review a certain number of possible targets per given length of time," *The Atlantic*'s Joshua Foust wrote of the private contractors involved in the process. "Because they are contractors," he explains, "their continued employment depends on their ability to satisfy the stated performance metrics. So they have a financial incentive to make life-or-death decisions about possible kill targets just to stay employed. This should be an intolerable situation, but because the system lacks transparency or outside review it is almost impossible to monitor or alter."

As flight hours rise year by year, these stark drawbacks are compounded by a series of technical glitches and vulnerabilities that are ever more regularly coming to light. Over the last decade, a more-is-better mentality has led to increased numbers of drones, drone bases, drone pilots, and drone victims, but not much else. Drones may be effective in terms of generating body counts, but they appear to be even more successful in generating animosity and creating enemies.

The Air Force's accident reports are replete with evidence of the flaws inherent in drone technology, and there can be little doubt that, in the future, ever more will come to light. A decade's worth of futility suggests that drone warfare itself may already be crashing and burning, yet it seems destined that the skies will fill with drones and that the future will bring more of the same.

An MQ-9 Reaper, armed with GBU-12 Paveway II laser guided munitions and AGM-114 Hellfire missiles, flies a combat mission over southern Afghanistan. (U.S. Air Force Photo / Lt. Col. Leslie Pratt)

Chapter 11

Remotely Piloted War

Tom Engelhardt

In the American mind, if Apple made weapons, they would undoubtedly be drones, those remotely piloted planes getting such great press here. They have generally been greeted as if they were the sleekest of iPhones armed with missiles.

When the first American drone assassins burst onto the global stage early in the last decade, they caught most of us by surprise, especially because they seemed to come out of nowhere or from some wild sci-fi novel. Ever since, they've been touted in the media as the shiniest presents under the American Christmas tree of war, the perfect weapons to solve our problems when it comes to evildoers lurking in the global badlands.

And can you blame Americans for their love affair with the drone? Who wouldn't be wowed by the most technologically advanced, futuristic, no-pain-all-gain weapon around?

Here's the thing, though: put drones in a more familiar context, skip the awestruck commentary, and they should have been eerily familiar. If, for instance, they were car

133

factories, they would seem so much less exotic to us.

Think about it: What does a drone do? Like a modern car factory, it replaces a pilot, a skilled job that takes significant training, with robotics and a degraded version of the same job outsourced elsewhere. In this case, the "offshore" location that job headed for wasn't China or Mexico, but a military base in the U.S., where a guy with a joystick, trained in a hurry and sitting at a computer monitor, is "piloting" that plane. And given our experience with the hemorrhaging of good jobs from the U.S., who will be surprised to discover that, in 2011, the U.S. Air Force was already training more drone "pilots" than actual fighter and bomber pilots combined?

That's one way drones are something other than the futuristic sci-fi wonders we imagine them to be. But there's another way that drones have been heading for the American "homeland" for four decades, and it has next to nothing to do with technology, advanced or otherwise.

In a sense, drone war might be thought of as the most natural form of war for the All Volunteer Military. To understand why that's so, we need to head back to a crucial decision implemented just as the Vietnam War was ending.

Disarming the Amateurs, Demobilizing the Citizenry

It's true that, in the wake of grinding wars that have also been debacles -- the Afghan version of which has entered its 11th year -- the U.S. military is in ratty shape. Its equipment needs refurbishing and its troops are worn down. The stress of endlessly repeated tours of duty in war zones, brain injuries and other wounds caused by the roadside bombs that have often replaced a visible enemy on the "battlefield," suicide rates that can't be staunched, rising sexual violence within the military, increasing crime rates around military bases, and all the other strains and pains of unending war have taken their toll.

Still, ours remains an intact, unrebellious, professional military. If you really want to see a force on its last legs, you need to leave the post-9/11 years behind and go back to the Vietnam era. In 1971, in *Armed Forces Journal*, Colonel Robert D. Heinl, Jr., author of a definitive history of the Marine Corps, wrote of "widespread conditions among American forces in Vietnam that have only been exceeded in this century by the French Army's Nivelle mutinies of 1917 and the collapse of the Tsarist armies [of Russia] in 1916 and 1917."

The U.S. military in Vietnam and at bases in the U.S. and around world was essentially at the edge of rebellion. Disaffection with an increasingly unpopular war on the Asian mainland, rejected by ever more Americans and emphatically protested at home, had infected the military, which was, after all, made up significantly of draftees.

Desertion rates were rising, as was drug use. In the field, "search and evade" (a mocking replacement for "search and destroy") operations were becoming commonplace. "Fraggings" -- attacks on unpopular officers or NCOs -- had doubled. "Word of the deaths of officers will bring cheers at troop movies or in bivouacs of certain units," wrote Col. Heinl, and according to him, there were then as many as 144 antiwar "underground newspapers" published by or aimed at soldiers. At the moment when he wrote, in fact, the antiwar movement in the U.S. was being spearheaded by a rising tide of disaffected Vietnam veterans speaking out against their war and the way they had fought it.

In this fashion, an American citizen's army, a draft military, had reached its limits and was voting with its feet against an imperial war. This was democracy in action transferred to the battlefield and the military base. And it was deeply disturbing to the U.S. high command, which had, by then, lost faith in the future possibilities of a draft army. In fact, faced with ever more ill-disciplined troops, the military's top commanders had clearly concluded: never again!

So on the very day the Paris Peace Accords were signed in January 1973, officially signaling the end of U.S. involvement in Vietnam (though not quite its actual end), President Richard Nixon also signed a decree ending the draft. It was an admission of the obvious: war, American-style, as it had been practiced since World War II, had lost its hold on young minds.

There was no question that U.S. military and civilian leaders intended, at that moment, to sever war and war-making from an aroused citizenry. In that sense, they glimpsed something of the future they meant to shape, but even they couldn't have guessed just where American war would be heading. Army Chief of Staff General Creighton Abrams, for instance, actually thought he was curbing the future rashness of civilian leaders by -- as Andrew Bacevich explained in his book *The New American Militarism* -- "making the active army operationally dependent on the reserves." In this way, no future president could commit the country to a significant war "without first taking the politically sensitive and economically costly step of calling up America's 'weekend warriors.'"

Abrams was wrong, of course, though he ensured that, decades hence, the reserves, too, would suffer the pain of disastrous wars once again fought on the Eurasian mainland. Still, whatever the generals and the civilian leaders didn't know about the effects of their acts then, the founding of the All-Volunteer Force (AVF) may have been the single most important decision made by Washington in the post-Vietnam era of the foreshortened American Century.

Today, few enough even remember that moment and far fewer have considered its import. Yet, historically speaking, that 1973 severing of war from the populace might be said to have ended an almost two-century-old democratic experiment in fusing the mobilized citizen and the mobilized state in wartime. It had begun with the *levée en masse* during the French Revolution, which sent roused citizens to the front to save the republic and spread their democratic fervor abroad. Behind them stood a mobilized population ready to sacrifice anything for the republic (and all too soon, of course, the empire).

It turned out, however, that the drafted citizen had his limits and so, almost 200 years later, another aroused citizenry and its soldiers, home front and war front, were to be pacified, to be put out to pasture, while the empire's wars were to be left to the professionals. An era was ending, even if no one noticed. (As a result, if you're in the mood to indulge in irony, citizen's war would be left to the guerrillas of the world, which in our era has largely meant to fundamentalist religious sects.)

Just calling in the professionals and ushering out the amateurs wasn't enough, though, to make the decision truly momentous. Another choice had to be married to it. The debacle that was Vietnam -- or what, as the 1970s progressed, began to be called "the Vietnam Syndrome" (as if the American people had been struck by some crippling psychic disease) -- could have sent Washington, and so the nation, off on another course entirely.

The U.S. could have retreated, however partially, from the world to lick its wounds. Instead, the country's global stance as the "leader of the free world" and its role as self-appointed global policeman were never questioned, nor was the global military basing policy that underlay it. In the midst of the Cold War, from Indonesia to Latin America, Japan to the Middle East, no diminution of U.S. imperial dreams was ever seriously considered.

The decision not to downsize its global military presence in the wake of Vietnam fused with the decision to create a military that would free Washington from worry about what the troops might think. Soon enough, as Bacevich wrote, the new AVF would be made up of "highly trained, handsomely paid professionals who (assuming that the generals concur with the wishes of the political leadership) will go anywhere without question to do the bidding of the commander-in-chief." It would, in fact, open the way for a new kind of militarism at home and abroad.

The Arrival of the Warrior Corporation

In the wake of Vietnam, the wars ceased and, for a few years, war even fled American popular culture. When it returned, the dogfights would be in outer space. (Think *Star Wars.*) In the meantime, a kind of stunned silence, a feeling of defeat, descended on the American polity -- but not for long. In the 1980s, the years of Ronald Reagan's presidency, American-style war was carefully rebuilt, this time to new specifications.

Reagan himself declared Vietnam "a noble cause," and a newly professionalized military, purged of malcontents and rebels, once again began invading small countries (Grenada, Panama). At the same time, the Pentagon was investing thought and planning into how to put the media (blamed for defeat in Vietnam) in its rightful place and so give the public the war news it deserved. In the process, reporters were first restrained from, then "pooled" in, and finally "embedded" in the war effort, while retired generals were sent into TV newsrooms like so many play-by-play analysts on *Monday Night Football* to narrate our wars as they were happening. Meanwhile, the public was simply sidelined.

Year by year, war became an ever more American activity and yet grew ever more remote from most Americans. The democratic citizen with a free mind and the ability to rebel had been sent home, and then demobilized on that home front as well. As a result, despite the endless post-9/11 gab about honoring and supporting the troops, a mobilized "home front" sacrificing for those fighting in their name would become a relic of history in a country whose leaders had begun boasting of having the greatest military the world had ever seen.

It wasn't, however, that no one was mobilizing. In the space vacated by the citizen, mobilization continued, just in a different fashion. Ever more mobilized, for instance, would be the powers of big science and the academy in the service of the Pentagon, the weapons makers, and the corporation.

Meanwhile, over the years, that "professional" army, that "all volunteer" force, began to change as well. From the 1990s on, in a way that would have been inconceivable for a draft army, it began to be privatized -- fused, that is, into the corporate way of war and profit.

War would now be fought not for or by the citizen, but quite literally for and by Lockheed Martin, Halliburton, KBR, DynCorp, Triple Canopy, and Blackwater (later Xe, even later Academi). Meanwhile, that citizen was to shudder at the thought of our terrorist enemies and then go on with normal life as if nothing whatsoever were happening. ("Get down to Disney World in Florida. Take your families and enjoy life the way we want it to be enjoyed," was George W. Bush's suggested response to the 9/11 attacks two weeks after they happened, with the "war on terror" already going on the books.)

Despite a paucity of real enemies of any substance, taxpayer dollars would pour into the coffers of the Pentagon and the military-industrial complex, as well as a new mini-homeland-security-industrial complex and a burgeoning intelligence-industrial complex, at levels unknown in the Cold War years. Lobbyists would be everywhere and the times would be the best, even when, in the war zones, things were going badly indeed.

Meanwhile, in those war zones, the Big Corporation would take over the humblest of soldierly roles -- the peeling of potatoes, the cooking of meals, the building of bases and outposts, the delivery of mail -- and it would take up the gun (and the bomb) as well. Soon enough, even the dying would be outsourced to corporate hirees. Occupied Iraq and Afghanistan would be flooded with tens of thousands of private contractors and hired guns, while military men trained in elite special operations units would find their big paydays by joining mercenary corporations doing similar work, often in the same war zones.

It was a remarkable racket. War and profit had long been connected in complicated ways, but seldom quite so straightforwardly. Now, win or lose on the battlefield, there would always be winners among the growing class of warrior corporations.

The All-Volunteer Force, pliant as a military should be, and backed by Madison Avenue to the tune of hundreds of millions of dollars to insure that its ranks were full, would become ever more detached from most of American society. It would, in fact, become ever more foreign (as in "foreign legion") and ever more mercenary (think Hessians). The intelligence services of the national security state would similarly outsource significant parts of their work to the private sector. According to Dana

Priest and William Arkin of the *Washington Post*, by 2010, about 265,000 of the 854,000 people with top security clearances were private contractors and "close to 30% of the workforce in the intelligence agencies [was] contractors."

No one seemed to notice, but a 1% version of American war was coming to fruition, unchecked by a draft Army, a skeptical Congress, or a democratic citizenry. In fact, Americans, generally preoccupied with lives in which our wars played next to no part, paid little attention.

Remotely Piloted War

Although early drone technology was already being used over North Vietnam, it's in another sense entirely that drones have been heading into America's future since 1973. There was an eerie logic to it: first came professional war, then privatized war, then mercenary and outsourced war -- all of which made war ever more remote from most Americans. Finally, both literally and figuratively, came remote war itself.

It couldn't be more appropriate that the Air Force prefers you not call their latest wonder weapons "unmanned aerial vehicles," or UAVs, anymore. They would like you to use the label "remotely piloted aircraft" (RPA) instead. And ever more remotely piloted that vehicle is to be, until -- claim believers and enthusiasts -- it will pilot itself, land itself, maneuver itself, and while in the air even choose its own targets.

In this sense, think of us as moving from the citizen's army to a roboticized, and finally robot, military -- to a military that is a foreign legion in the most basic sense. In other words, we are moving toward an ever greater outsourcing of war to things that cannot protest, cannot vote with their feet (or wings), and for whom there is no "home front" or even a home at all. In a sense, we are, as we have been since 1973, heading for a form of war without anyone, citizen or otherwise, in the picture -- except those on the ground, enemy and civilian alike, who will die as usual.

Of course, it may never happen this way, in part because drones are anything but wonder weapons, and in part because corporate war fought by a thoroughly professional military turns out to be staggeringly expensive to the demobilized citizen, profligate in its waste, and -- by the evidence of recent history -- remarkably unsuccessful. It also couldn't be more remote from the idea of a democracy or a republic.

In a sense, the modern imperial age began hundreds of years ago with corporate war, when Dutch, British and other East India companies set sail, armed to the teeth, to subdue the world at a profit. Perhaps corporate war will also prove the end point for that age, the perfect formula for the last global empire on its way down.

Chapter 12

A Drone-Eat-Drone World

Nick Turse

U.S. military documents tell the story vividly. In the Gulf of Guinea, off the coast of West Africa, an unmanned mini-submarine deployed from the USS *Freedom* detects an "anomaly": another small remotely-operated sub with welding capabilities tampering with a major undersea oil pipeline. The American submarine's "smart software" classifies the action as a possible threat and transmits the information to an unmanned drone flying overhead. The robot plane begins collecting intelligence data and is soon circling over a nearby vessel, a possible "mother ship," suspected of being involved with the "remote welder."

At a hush-hush "joint maritime operations center" onshore, analysts pour over digital images captured by the unmanned sub and, according to a Pentagon report, recognize the welding robot "as one recently stolen and acquired by rebel antigovernment forces." An elite quick-reaction force is assembled at a nearby airfield and dispatched to the scene, while a second unmanned drone is deployed to provide persistent surveillance of the area of operations.

And with that, the drone war is on.

At the joint maritime operations center, signals intelligence analysts detect the mother ship launching a Russian Tipchak -- a medium-altitude, long-endurance, unmanned aircraft with "U.S.-derived systems and avionics" and outfitted with air-to-air as well as air-to-surface missiles. It's decision time for U.S. commanders. Special Operations Forces are already en route and, with an armed enemy drone in the skies ahead of them, possibly in peril.

But the Americans have an ace up their sleeve: an advanced Air Force MQ-1000. Unlike the MQ-1 Predator and the MQ-9 Reaper, the MQ-1000 is capable of completely autonomous action, right down to targeting and combat.

Pre-programmed with the requirements and constraints of the mission, the advanced drone takes off and American commanders let it do its thing. "The MQ-1000… immediately conducts an air-to-air engagement and neutralizes the Tipchak," reads the understated official account of the action. The special ops team then raids the mothership and disrupts the oil pipeline interdiction scheme.

The entire episode involves a seamless integration of robots and troops working in tandem, of next-generation drones "wired" together and operating in teams, and of autonomous drones making their own decisions. But there's a reason you've never read about this mission in the *New York Times* or the *Washington Post*. It won't take place for 20 years.

Or will it?

The "African Maritime Coalition Vignette, 2030s," is a scenario offered up in *Unmanned Systems Integrated Roadmap, FY 2011-2036*, a recently released 100-page Defense Department document outlining American robotic air, sea, and land war-fighting plans for the decades ahead. It's the sunny side of a future once depicted in the *Terminator* films in which flying hunter-killer or "HK" units are sent out to exterminate the human race.

Terminators of Today?

In some ways, of course, the future is now. When the first *Terminator* movie was released in 1984, its HKs seemed as futuristic as its time-traveling cyborg title-character. Nearly three decades later, we're living in an age in which armed robots do regularly surveil, track, and kill people. But instead of a self-aware computer network known as Skynet, it's the American president or his intelligence officials and military officers who determine the human targets to be terminated by unmanned hunter-killer craft.

Washington's post-9/11 military interventions have been a boon for drones. The numbers tell the story. At the turn of this century, the Department of Defense had 90 drones with plans to increase the inventory by 200 over the next decade, according to Dyke Weatherington, a Defense Department deputy director overseeing acquisitions of hardware for unmanned warfare. As 2012 began, there were more than 9,500 RPAs in the U.S. arsenal.

Today, the Army, Navy, Air Force, Marines, and Special Operations Command all field drones with names that sound as if they were ripped from a Hollywood script or a comic book: Sentinel, Avenger, Wasp, Raven, Puma, Shadow, Scan Eagle, Global Hawk, Hunter, Gray Eagle, Predator, and Reaper. The latter three, *Unmanned Systems Integrated Roadmap* notes, "are weaponized to conduct offensive operations, irregular warfare, and high-value target/high value individual prosecution, and this trend will likely continue."

The Air Force's MQ-1 Predator has been the workhorse of America's hunter-killer drone fleet. By the end of 2001, Predators had cumulatively flown 25,000 hours. By this March, according to statistics provided by the Air Force, they had logged 1,127,400 flight hours, 1,041,740 of them in combat.

The military quit buying Predators in 2010, opting instead for the larger, more heavily armed Reaper. These have flown more than 261,000 hours, including 228,000 in combat. The Air Force has already requested the purchase of 24 new Reapers in 2013 and Air Force spokesperson Jennifer Spires tells

TomDispatch it plans to buy a grand total of 401 MQ-9s in the coming years.

In other ways, however, a sci-fi-style future is far off indeed. In fact, after a decade of Defense Department cheerleading, as well as endless TV and newspaper puff pieces on the unlimited potential of drone technology, a grimmer and dimmer future for them is coming into view.

As a start, most of the drones in the Pentagon's inventory aren't sophisticated hunter-killer robots, but smaller, unarmed tactical models used only for battlefield surveillance. According to figures provided to TomDispatch by the Army, that service has approximately 5,000 drones, about 1,400 of them currently supporting operations in Afghanistan (where one of their key models, the Shadow, collided with a cargo plane last year). While it has plans to arm increasing numbers of its larger models with munitions, they're hardly the stuff of Hollywood sci-fi flicks.

Even the Predator and Reaper are little more than expensive, error-prone, overgrown model airplanes remotely "flown" by all-too-human pilots. They tend to crash at an alarming rate due to weather, mechanical failures, and computer glitches, leaving shattered silver-screen techno-dreams of cheap, error-free, futuristic warfare in the dust.

Today's armed drones are actually the weak sisters of the weapons world. Even the Reaper is slow, clumsy, unarmored, generally unable to perceive threats around it, and -- writes defense expert Winslow Wheeler -- "fundamentally incapable of defending itself." While Reapers have been outfitted with missiles for theoretical air-to-air combat capabilities, those armaments would be functionally useless in a real-world dogfight.

Similarly, in a 2011 report, the Air Force Scientific Advisory Board admitted that modern air defense systems "would quickly decimate the current Predator/Reaper fleet and be a serious threat against the high-flying Global Hawk." Unlike that MQ-1000 of 2030, today's top drone would be a sitting duck if any reasonably armed enemy wanted to take it on. In this sense, as in many others, it compares unfavorably to current manned combat aircraft.

The Navy's even newer MQ-8B Fire Scout, a much-hyped drone helicopter that has been tested as a weapons platform, has also gone bust. Not only was one shot down in Libya last year, but repeated crashes have caused the Navy to ground the robo-copter "for the indefinite future."

Even the highly classified RQ-170 Sentinel couldn't stay airborne over Iran during a secret mission that suddenly became very public last year. Whether or not an Iranian attack brought down the drone, the Air Force Scientific Advisory Board report makes it clear that there are numerous methods by which remotely piloted aircraft can potentially be thwarted or downed from the use of lasers and dazzlers to blind or damage sensors to simple jammers to disrupt global positioning systems to a wide range of cyber-attacks, the jamming of commercial satellite communications, and the spoofing or hijacking of drone data links.

Smaller tactical unmanned aircraft may be even more susceptible to low-tech attacks, not to mention constrained in their abilities and cumbersome to use. Sergeant Christopher Harris, an Army drone pilot and infantryman, described the limitations of the larger of the two hand-launched drones he's operated in Afghanistan this way: the 13-pound Puma was best used from an observation post with some elevation; it only had a 12-mile range and, though theoretically possible to take on patrol, was "a beast to carry around" once the weight of extra batteries and equipment was factored in.

Terminators of Tomorrow?

As for the future, the Air Force's 2011-2036 *Roadmap* has already hit a major detour. In 2010, *Air Force* magazine breathlessly announced, "Early in the next decade, the Air Force will deploy a new, stealthy RPA -- currently called the MQ-X -- capable of surviving in heavily defended airspace and performing a wide variety of ISR [*intelligence, surveillance, reconnaissance]* and strike missions."
Indeed, the 2011 *Roadmap* lists the MQ-X as the future of Air Force drones. In February

2012 however, Lieutenant General Larry James told an *Aviation Week*-sponsored conference: "At this point... we don't plan, in the near term, to invest in any sort of MQ-X like program." Instead, James said, the Air Force will be content simply to upgrade the Reaper fleet and watch the Navy's development of its Unmanned Carrier-Launched Airborne Surveillance and Strike or UCLASS drone to see if it soars or, like so many RPAs, crashes and burns.

The Holy Grail of drone ops is the ability of an aircraft to linger over suspected target areas for long durations. But ultra-long-term loitering operations still remain in the realm of fantasy. Admittedly, the Pentagon's blues skies research arm, the Defense Advanced Research Projects Agency, is pursuing an ambitious drone project to provide intelligence, surveillance, reconnaissance, and "communication missions over an area of interest" for five or more years at a time. The project, dubbed "Vulture," is meant to provide satellite-like capabilities "in an aircraft package."

Right now, it sounds downright unlikely.

While the Air Force has had a hush-hush unmanned space plane orbiting the Earth for more than a year, much like a standard satellite, the longest a U.S. military drone has reportedly stayed aloft within the planet's atmosphere is a little more than 336 hours. Plans for ultra-long duration flights took a major hit last year, according to scientists at Sandia National Laboratories and defense giant Northrop Grumman.

In an effort to "to increase UAV [unmanned aerial vehicle] sortie duration from days to months while increasing available electrical power at least two-fold," according to a 2011 report made public by the Federation of American Scientists's Secrecy News, the Sandia and Northrop Grumman researchers identified a technology that "would have provided system performance unparalleled by other existing technologies." In a year in which the Fukushima Daiichi nuclear disaster turned a swath of Japan into an irradiated no-go zone, the use of that mystery technology, never named in the report but assumed to be nuclear power, was deemed untenable due to "current political conditions."

With the Pentagon now lobbying the Federal Aviation Administration to open U.S. airspace to its robotic aircraft and ever more articles emerging about drone crashes, don't bet on nuclear-powered, long-loitering drones appearing any time soon, nor for many of the other major promised innovations in Drone World to come online in the near term either.

From Dystopian Fiction to Dystopian Reality

Until recently, drones looked like a can't-miss technology primed for big budget increases and revolutionary advances, but all that's changing fast. "Realistic expectations are for zero growth in the unmanned systems funding," Weatherington explained by email. "Most increases will be in technical innovations improving application of delivered systems on the battlefield, and driving down the cost of ownership."

Major Jeffrey Poquette of the Army's Small Unmanned Air Systems Product Office talked about just such an effort. By the late summer, he said, the Army planned to introduce more sophisticated sensors, including the ability to track targets more easily, in its four-pound Raven surveillance drones. Put less politely, what this means is no roll-outs of sophisticated new drone systems or revolutionary new drone technology; the Army will simply upgrade a glorified model airplane that first took flight more than a decade ago.

Sci-fi it isn't, but that doesn't mean that nothing will change in the world of drone warfare.

The *Terminator* films weren't exactly original in predicting a future of unmanned planes dominating the world's skies. At the end of World War II, General Henry "Hap" Arnold of the U.S. Army Air Forces praised American pilots for their wartime performance, but suggested their days might be numbered. "The next war may be fought by airplanes with no men in them at all," he explained. The future of combat aviation, he announced, would be "different from anything the world has ever seen."

The most salient and accurate of Arnold's predictions was not, however, his forecast about drone warfare. Pilotless planes had taken flight years before the Wright Brothers launched their manned airplane at Kitty Hawk, North Carolina, in 1903, and drones would not become a signature piece of American weaponry until the 2000s. Instead, Arnold's faith in a "next war" -- a clear departure from the sentiments of so many Americans after World War I -- proved accurate again and again. Over the following decades, American aircraft would strike in North Korea, South Korea, Indonesia, Guatemala, Cuba, North Vietnam, South Vietnam, Laos, Cambodia, Grenada, Libya, Panama, Iraq, Kuwait, the former Yugoslavia, Afghanistan, Yemen, Iraq (again), Pakistan, Somalia, Yemen (again), Libya (again), and the Philippines. New technologies came and went, air strikes were the constant.

In Vietnam, the former Yugoslavia, Afghanistan, Iraq, Pakistan, Yemen, Somalia, Libya, and the Philippines, the U.S. deployed pilotless planes as per Arnold's other prediction. From Afghanistan onward, all of the countries that have experienced American air power have also experienced lethal drone attacks -- just how many is unknown because figures on drone strikes are kept secret "for security reasons," the Air Force's Spires recently told TomDispatch. What we do know is that drone attacks have increased radically over the years. "More" has been the name of the game.

Still, barely a decade after our drone wars began, dreams of *Terminatoresque* efficiency and technological perfection are all but dead, even if the drone itself is increasingly embedded in our world. Fantasies of autonomous drones and submarines fighting robot wars off the coast of Africa are already fading for any near-term future. But drone warfare is here to stay. Count on drones to be an essential part of the American way of war for a long time to come.

Air Force contracting documents suggest that the estimated five Reaper sorties flown each day in 2012 will jump to 66 per day by 2016. What that undoubtedly means is more countries with drones flying over them, more drone bases, more crashes, more mistakes. What we're unlikely to see is armed drones scoring decisive military victories, offering solutions to complex foreign-policy problems, or even providing an answer to the issue of terrorism, despite the hopes of policymakers and the military brass.
Keep in mind as well that those global skies are going to fill with the hunter-killer drones of other nations in what could soon enough become a drone-eat-drone world. With that still largely in the future, however, the Pentagon continues to glow with enthusiasm over the advantages drones offer the U.S.

Regarding the importance of military robots, for instance, the Pentagon's Dyke Weatherington explained, "Combatant commanders and warfighters place value in the inherent features of unmanned systems -- especially their persistence, versatility, and reduced risk to human life."

On that last point, of course, Weatherington is only thinking about American military personnel and American lives. Tomorrow's drone warfare will likely mean "more" in one other area: more dead civilians. We've left behind the fiction of Hollywood for a less high-tech but distinctly dystopian reality. It isn't quite the movies and it isn't what the Pentagon mapped out, but it indisputably provides a clear path to a grim and grimy Terminator Planet.

Postscript

America as a Shining Drone Upon a Hill

Tom Engelhardt

Here's the essence of it: you can trust America's *crème de la crème*, the most elevated, responsible people, no matter what weapons, what powers, you put in their hands. No need to constantly look over *their* shoulders.

Placed in the hands of evildoers, those weapons and powers could create a living nightmare; controlled by the best of people, they lead to measured, thoughtful, precise decisions in which bad things are (with rare and understandable exceptions) done only to truly terrible types. In the process, you simply couldn't be better protected.

And in case you were wondering, there is no question who among us are the best, most lawful, moral, ethical, considerate, and judicious people: the officials of our national security state. Trust them implicitly. They will never give you a bum steer.

You may be paying a fortune to maintain their world -- the 30,000 people hired to listen in on conversations and other communications in this country, the 230,000 employees of the Department of Homeland Security, the 854,000

158

people with top-secret clearances, the 4.2 million with security clearances of one sort or another, the $2 billion, one-million-square-foot data center that the National Security Agency is constructing in Utah, the gigantic $1.8 billion headquarters the National Geospatial Intelligence Agency recently built for its 16,000 employees in the Washington area -- but there's a good reason. That's what's needed to make truly elevated, surgically precise decisions about life and death in the service of protecting American interests on this dangerous globe of ours.

And in case you wondered just how we know all this, we have it on the best authority: the people who are doing it -- the only ones, given the obvious need for secrecy, capable of judging just how moral, elevated, and remarkable their own work is. They deserve our congratulations, but if we're too distracted to give it to them, they are quite capable of high-fiving themselves.

We're talking, in particular, about the use by the Obama administration (and the Bush administration before it) of a growing armada of grimly labeled Predators and Reaper drones to fight a nameless, almost planet-wide war (formerly known as the Global War on Terror). Its purpose: to destroy al-Qaeda-in-wherever and all its wannabes and look-alikes, the Taliban, and anyone affiliated or associated with any of the above, or just about anyone else we believe might imminently endanger our "interests."

In the service of this war, in the midst of a perpetual state of war and of wartime, every act committed by these leaders is, it turns out, absolutely, totally, and completely legal. We have their say-so for that, and they have the documents to prove it, largely because the best and most elevated legal minds among them have produced that documentation in secret. (Of course, they dare not show it to the rest of us, lest lives be endangered.)

By their own account, they have, in fact, been covertly exceptional, moral, and legal for more than a decade (minus, of course, the odd black site and torture chamber) -- so covertly exceptional, in fact, that they haven't quite gotten the credit they deserve. Now, they would like to make the latest version of their exceptional mission to the world known to the rest of us. It is finally in our interest, it seems, to be a good deal better informed about America's covert wars in a year in which the widely announced "covert" killing of Osama bin Laden in Pakistan is a major selling point in the president's reelection campaign.

No one should be surprised. There was always an "overt" lurking in the "covert" of what now passes for "covert war." The CIA's global drone assassination campaign has long been a bragging point in Washington, even if it couldn't officially be discussed directly before, say, Congress. The covertness of our drone wars in the Pakistani tribal borderlands, Somalia, Yemen, and elsewhere really turns out to have less to do with secrecy -- just about every covert drone strike is reported, sooner or later, in the media -- than assuring two administrations that they could pursue their drone wars without accountability to anyone.

A Classic of Self-Congratulation

In May 2012, top administration officials began fanning out to offer rare peeks into what's truly on-target and exceptional about America's drone wars. In many ways, these days, American exceptionalism is about as unexceptional as apple pie. It has, for one thing, become the everyday language of the presidential campaign trail. And that shouldn't surprise us either. After all, great powers and their leaders tend to think well of themselves. The French had their "*mission civilisatrice*," the Chinese had the "mandate of heaven," and like all imperial powers they inevitably thought they were doing the best for themselves and others, sadly benighted, in this best of all possible worlds.

Sometimes, though, the American version of this does seem... I hate to use the word, but exceptional. If you want to get a taste of just what this means, consider as Exhibit One a May speech by the president's counterterrorism "tsar," John Brennan, at the Woodrow Wilson International Center for Scholars. According to his own account, he was dispatched to the center by President Obama to provide greater openness when it comes to the administration's secret drone wars, to respond to critics of the drones and their legality, and undoubtedly to put a smiley face on drone operations generally.

Ever since the Puritan minister John Winthrop first used the phrase in a sermon on shipboard on the way to North America, "a city upon a hill" has caught something of at least one American-style dream -- a sense that this country's fate was to be a blessed paragon for the rest of the world, an exception to every norm. In the last century, it became "a shining city upon a hill" and was regularly cited in presidential addresses.

Whatever that "city," that dream, was once imagined to be, it has undergone a largely unnoticed metamorphosis in the twenty-first century. It has become -- even in our dreams -- an up-armored garrison encampment, just as Washington itself has become the heavily fortified bureaucratic heartland of a war state. So when Brennan spoke, what he offered was a new version of American exceptionalism: the first "shining drone upon a hill" speech, which also qualifies as an instant classic of self-congratulation.

Never, according to him, has a country with such an advanced weapon system as the drone used it quite so judiciously, quite so -- if not peacefully -- at least with the sagacity and skill usually reserved for the gods. American drone strikes, he assured his listeners, are "ethical and just," "wise," and "surgically precise" -- exactly what you'd expect from a country he refers to, quoting the president, as *the* preeminent "standard bearer in the conduct of war."

Those drone strikes, he added, are based on staggeringly "rigorous standards" involving the individual identification of human targets. Even when visited on American citizens outside declared war zones, they are invariably "within the bounds of the law," as you would expect of the preeminent "nation of laws."

The strikes are never motivated by vengeance, always target someone known to us as the worst of the worst, and almost invariably avoid anyone who is even the most mediocre of the mediocre. (Forget the fact that, as Greg Miller of the *Washington Post* reported in late April, the CIA has received permission from the president to launch drone strikes in Yemen based only on the observed "patterns of suspicious behavior" of groups of unidentified individuals, as was already true in the Pakistani tribal borderlands.)

Yes, in such circumstances innocents do unfortunately die, even if unbelievably rarely -- and for that we couldn't be more regretful. Such deaths, however, are in some sense salutary, since they lead to the most rigorous reviews and reassessments of, and so improvements in, our actions. "This too," Brennan assured his audience, "is a reflection of our values as Americans."

"I would note," he added, "that these standards, for identifying a target and avoiding... the loss of lives of innocent civilians, exceed what is required as a matter of international law on a typical battlefield. That's another example of the high standards to which we hold ourselves."

And that's just a taste of the tone and substance of the speech given by the president's leading counterterrorism expert, and in it he's no outlier. It catches something about an American sense of self at this moment. Yes, Americans may be ever more down on the Afghan war, but like their leaders, they are high on drones. In a February *Washington Post*/ABC News poll, 83% of respondents supported the administration's use of drones. Perhaps that's not surprising either, since the drones are generally presented here as the coolest of machines, as well as cheap alternatives (in money and lives) to sending more armies onto the Eurasian mainland.

Predator Nation

In these last years, this country has pioneered the development of the most advanced killing machines on the planet for which the national security state has plans decades into the future. Conceptually speaking, our leaders have also established their "right" to send these robot assassins into any airspace, no matter the local claims of national sovereignty, to take out those we define as evil or simply to protect American interests. On this, Brennan couldn't be clearer. In the process, we have turned much of the rest of the planet into what can only be considered an American free-fire zone.

We have, in short, established a remarkably expansive set of drone-war rules for the global future. Naturally, we trust ourselves with such rules, but there *is* a fly in the ointment, even as the droniacs see it. Others far less sagacious, kindly, lawful, and good than we are do exist on this planet and they may soon have their own fleets of drones. About 50 countries are today buying or developing such robotic aircraft, including Russia, China, and Iran, not to speak of Hezbollah in Lebanon. And who knows what terror groups are looking into suicide drones?

As the *Washington Post's* David Ignatius put it in a column about Brennan's speech: "What if the Chinese deployed drones to protect their workers in southern Sudan against rebels who have killed them in past attacks? What if Iran used them against Kurdish separatists they regard as terrorists? What if Russia used them over Chechnya? What position would the United States take, and wouldn't it be hypocritical if it opposed drone attacks by other nations that face 'imminent' or 'significant' threats?"

This is Washington's global drone conundrum as seen from inside the Beltway. These are the nightmarish scenarios even our leaders can imagine *others* producing with their own drones and our rules. A deeply embedded sense of American exceptionalism, a powerful belief in their own special, self-evident goodness, however, conveniently blinds them to what they are doing right now. Looking in the mirror, they are incapable of seeing a mask of death. And yet our proudest export at present, other than Hollywood superhero films, may be a stone-cold robotic killer with a name straight out of a horror movie.

Consider this as well: those "shining drones" launched on campaigns of assassination and slaughter are increasingly the "face" that we choose to present to the world. And yet it's beyond us why it might not shine for others.

In reality, it's not so hard to imagine what we increasingly look like to those others: a Predator nation. And not just to the parents and relatives of the more than 160 children the Bureau of Investigative Journalism has documented as having died in U.S. drone strikes in Pakistan. After all, war is now the only game in town. Peace? For the managers of our national security state, it's neither a word worth mentioning, nor an imaginable condition.

In truth, our leaders should be in mourning for whatever peaceful dreams we ever had. But mention drones and they light up. They're having a love affair with those machines. They just can't get enough of them or imagine their world or ours without them.

What they can't see in the haze of exceptional self-congratulation is this: they are transforming the promise of America into a promise of death. And death, visited from the skies, isn't precise. It isn't glorious. It isn't judicious. It certainly isn't a shining vision. It's hell. And it's a global future for which, someday, no one will thank us.

A Note on the Text

The 12 chapters and postscript of this book on drones, written between April 2009 and May 2012, all appeared at the website TomDispatch.com that Tom Engelhardt and Nick Turse run. They were edited, sometimes modestly updated and trimmed of the telltale signs of the immediate moment -- all the "recentlys" and "next weeks" have been removed, along with a few thematic repetitions. Otherwise they remain as they appeared. For the record, and in case readers should wish to check out any of the essays in their original form at TomDispatch.com, below is a list of them with the dates they were posted, their full original titles, and their urls.

Chapter 1: *Terminator Planet, Launching the Drone Wars*, April 7, 2009
http://www.tomdispatch.com/post/175056.

Chapter 2: *Drone Race to a Known Future, Why Military Dreams Fail -- and Why It Doesn't Matter*, November 10, 2009
http://www.tomdispatch.com/post/175155.

Chapter 3: *The Drone Surge, Today, Tomorrow, and 2047*, January 24, 2010
http://www.tomdispatch.com/archive/175195/.

Chapter 4: *America Detached From War, Bush's Pilotless Dream, Smoking Drones, and Other Strange Tales From the Crypt*, June 24, 2010
http://www.tomdispatch.com/archive/175265/.

Chapter 5: *Taking the "War" Out of Air War, What U.S. Air Power Actually Does*, March 17, 2011
http://www.tomdispatch.com/archive/175368/.

Chapter 6: *America's Secret Empire of Drone Bases, Its Full Extent Revealed for the First Time*, October 16, 2011
http://www.tomdispatch.com/archive/175454/.

Chapter 7: *Sex and the Single Drone, The Latest in Guarding the Empire*, September 29, 2011
http://www.tomdispatch.com/blog/175447/.

Chapter 8: *The Drone That Fell From the Sky, What a Busted Robot Airplane Tells Us About the American Empire in 2012 and Beyond*, December 20, 2011
http://www.tomdispatch.com/blog/175482/.

Chapter 9: *Offshore Everywhere, How Drones, Special Operations Forces, and the U.S. Navy Plan to End National Sovereignty as We Know It*, February 5, 2012
http://www.tomdispatch.com/archive/175498/.

Chapter 10: *The Crash and Burn Future of Robot Warfare, What 70 Downed Drones Tell Us About the New American Way of War*, January 15, 2012
http://www.tomdispatch.com/post/175489/.

Chapter 11: *Remotely Piloted War, How Drone*

War Became the American Way of Life,
February 23, 2012
www.tomdispatch.com/post/175507/.

This book has no citations. The original posts at TomDispatch.com were, however, heavily footnoted in the style of the Internet -- through links that led readers to our sources and also sometimes offered directions for further exploration. Linking is the first democratic form of footnoting, making sources instantly accessible to normal readers who, unlike scholars, may not have ready access to a good library. URLs in a book, however, are both cumbersome and useless. So if you want to check our sources, you'll need to go to the originals online at TomDispatch.com. Fair warning, however: one of the debits of linking is that links regularly die, so the older the piece, the greater the chance that some of the links won't work.

The photos in this book were all provided by the U.S. Department of Defense.

Acknowledgments

Among the great myths is the solitariness of the writing enterprise. Every acknowledgments section makes mockery of the very idea. In the case of this book, already joined at the hip, we want to offer copious thanks to the crew who have made this whole enterprise possible from start to finish: Taya Kitman and Andy Breslau of the Nation Institute, who helped pave the way; Christopher Holmes, Andy Kroll, and Zoë Carpenter, who saved us from untold small errors; Jon Livingston, who gave us The Look; Joe Duax and Dimitri Siavelis, who kept us afloat in the Internet universe; Ann Jones, who urged us to do this in the first place; all the TomDispatch writers, who have offered us an ongoing education and a vivid sense of the world in which the drones now fly; Lannan Foundation, which has supported us and kept us afloat in a perilous world; and above all, our wives, Nancy Garrity and Tam Turse, who make life worth living. (An extra bow to Maggie and Will – of course.)

About Nick Turse

Nick Turse is an award-winning journalist, historian, essayist, and the associate editor of the Nation Institute's TomDispatch.com. He is the editor of *The Case for Withdrawal from Afghanistan* (Verso, 2010) and the author of *The Complex: How the Military Invades Our Everyday Lives* (Metropolitan Books/Henry Holt, 2008). His *Kill Anything That Moves: The Real American War in Vietnam* will be published by Metropolitan Books in 2013.

A national security reporter and historian of the Vietnam War, Turse has written for *The Los Angeles Times, The San Francisco Chronicle*, *The Nation, Adbusters*, *GOOD*, *Le Monde Diplomatique* (English- and German-language)*, In These Times, Mother Jones* and *The Village Voice*, among other print and on-line publications.

Turse, who holds a Ph.D in Sociomedical Sciences from Columbia University, was the recipient of a Ridenhour Prize for Investigative

Reporting at the National Press Club in April 2009 and a James Aronson Award for Social Justice Journalism from Hunter College. He has previously been awarded a Guggenheim fellowship as well as fellowships at New York University's Center for the United States and the Cold War, and Harvard University's Radcliffe Institute for Advanced Study. He has also received grants from the Fund for Investigative Journalism and the Pulitzer Center for Crisis Reporting.

He is married to Tam Turse, a photographer with whom he has collaborated on several reporting projects.

About Tom Engelhardt

Tom Engelhardt created and runs the TomDispatch.com website, a project of the Nation Institute, where he is a fellow. He is the author of two collections of his TomDispatch columns, *The United States of Fear* and *The American Way of War: How Bush's Wars Became Obama's*, as well as *The End of Victory Culture*, a highly praised history of American triumphalism in the Cold War, and *The Last Days of Publishing*, a novel. Many of his TomDispatch interviews were collected in *Mission Unaccomplished: TomDispatch Interviews with American Iconoclasts and Dissenters*. He also edited *The World According to TomDispatch: America in the New Age of Empire*, a collection of pieces from his site that functioned as an alternative history of the mad Bush years.

TomDispatch is the sideline that ate his life. Before creating it he worked as an editor at Pacific News Service in the early 1970s, and, these last four decades, as an editor in book publishing. For 15 years he was senior editor at Pantheon Books, where he edited and published award-winning works ranging from Art Spiegelman's *Maus* and John Dower's *War Without Mercy* to Eduardo Galeano's *Memory of Fire* trilogy. He is now consulting editor at Metropolitan Books, as well as the cofounder and coeditor of the American Empire Project (Metropolitan Books), where he has published best-selling works by Andrew Bacevich, Noam Chomsky, and Chalmers Johnson, among others. Many of the authors whose books he has edited and published over the years now write for TomDispatch.com. For a number of years, he was also a teaching fellow at the Graduate School of Journalism at the University of California, Berkeley. He is married to Nancy J. Garrity, a therapist, and has two children, Maggie and Will.

About TomDispatch

Tom Engelhardt launched
TomDispatch.com in October 2001 as
an email publication offering
commentary and collected articles from
the world press. In December 2002, it
gained its name, became a project of
the Nation Institute, and went online as
"a regular antidote to the mainstream
media." The site now features three
articles a week, all original. These
include Engelhardt's regular
commentaries as well as the work of
authors ranging from Rebecca Solnit,
Bill McKibben, Andrew Bacevich,
Barbara Ehrenreich, and Mike Davis to
Michael Klare, Adam Hochschild, Noam
Chomsky, and Karen J. Greenberg. Nick
Turse, who also writes for the site, is its
associate editor and research director.
Andy Kroll is an associate editor and the
site's economic correspondent. Timothy
MacBain produces regular TomCast
audio interviews with TomDispatch
authors and Erika Eichelberger handles
the site's social media. Christopher
Holmes is its eagle-eyed proofreader.
TomDispatch is intended to introduce
readers to voices and perspectives from
elsewhere (even when the elsewhere is

here). Its mission is to connect some of the global dots regularly left unconnected by the mainstream media and to offer a clearer sense of how this imperial globe of ours actually works.

About Dispatch Books

As an editor at Pantheon Books in the 1970s and 1980s, Tom Engelhardt used to jokingly call himself publishing's "editor of last resort." His urge to rescue books and authors rejected elsewhere brought the world Eduardo Galeano's beautiful *Memory of Fire* trilogy and Art Spiegelman's Pulitzer Prize-winning *Maus*, among other notable, incendiary, and worthy works. In that spirit, he and award-winning journalist Nick Turse founded Dispatch Books, a digital publishing effort offering a home for authors used to operating outside the mainstream.

With an eye for well-crafted essays, illuminating long-form investigative journalism, and compelling subjects given short-shrift by the big publishing houses, Engelhardt and Turse seek to provide readers with electronic books of conspicuous quality which offer unique perspectives found nowhere else. In a world in which publishing giants take fewer and fewer risks and style regularly trumps substance, Dispatch Books aims to be the informed reader's last refuge for uncommon voices, new perspectives, and provocative critiques. *Terminator Planet* launches it into the world.

1817654R00096

Made in the USA
San Bernardino, CA
04 February 2013